# Relaxing on the Porch

# Relaxing on the Porch

Megan Fulweiler

**FRIEDMAN/FAIRFAX**
PUBLISHERS

A FRIEDMAN/FAIRFAX BOOK

© 2000 by Michael Friedman Publishing Group, Inc.

Please visit our website: www.metrobooks.com

Library of Congress Cataloging-in-Publication Data

Fulweiler, Megan.
    Relaxing on the Porch / Megan Fulweiler.
        p. cm.
    ISBN 1-58663-034-2
        1. Porches—Design and construction.   2. Architecture, Domestic—20th century.   I. Title.

TH4970 .F85 2000
747—dc21

00-037598

Editor: Hallie Einhorn
Art Director: Jeff Batzli
Designer: Carole Goodman
Photography Editor: Kathleen Wolfe
Production Manager: Karen Matsu Greenberg

Color separations by Dai Nippon
Printed in Hong Kong by Dai Nippon Printing Company Limited

1 3 5 7 9 10 8 6 4 2

Distributed by Sterling Publishing Company, Inc.
387 Park Avenue South
New York, NY 10016
Distributed in Canada by Sterling Publishing
Canadian Manda Group
One Atlantic Avenue, Suite 105
Toronto, Ontario, Canada M6K 3E7
Distributed in Australia by
Capricorn Link (Australia) Pty Ltd.
P.O. Box 6651
Baulkham Hills, Business Centre, NSW 2153, Australia

*To John*

# Contents

*Introduction* . . . 8

CHAPTER ONE
*Timeless Appeal* . . . 12

CHAPTER TWO
*Sitting a Spell* . . . 28

CHAPTER THREE
*Basking in Privacy* . . . 60

CHAPTER FOUR
*Dining Alfresco* . . . 90

CHAPTER FIVE
*Tending the Porch Garden* . . . 126

*Source Directory* . . . 158

*Index* . . . 160

ABOVE: *Wicker chairs complement the elaborate architectural detailing of this Victorian porch. Somewhat removed from the hustle and bustle, the space is a peaceful oasis on a sultry afternoon.*

OPPOSITE: *Overlooking the water, this breezy porch affords occupants a tranquil view that is sure to put them at ease. The sense of relaxation is further promoted by a pair of cushioned rockers.*

# Introduction

F YOU TAKE A MOMENT TO SIFT THROUGH SOME OF YOUR MOST treasured memories, most likely you'll come across a special porch. It may be a grandmother's welcoming front porch, the back porch of a lakeside cottage that was home one summer, or perhaps a side porch that invited a stolen moment of privacy. To linger over these images is a pleasure, to discover porches anew is sheer bliss.

Whether rural or urban, traditional or contemporary, porches speak to relaxation and leisure. The size doesn't matter; even the smallest one can seem a utopia at the end of a busy day. A deep breath, feet up on the railing, a cool drink, and we are close to paradise.

No matter what the style—bungalow or Victorian, screened or open-air—a porch extends our living space. It not only affords us the opportunity to undertake a number of activities, but also keeps us connected to nature. Soaking in the landscape or enjoying the fellowship of friends, we are more at peace on the porch than anywhere else. It's from here that we'll watch the days lengthen, then shorten. We'll welcome guests, tote out sandwiches for the baseball team, maybe wave good-bye to a school-bound child for the first time. Greetings, departures, spur-of-the-moment meals, long delicious hours of doing absolutely, positively nothing—porches are the stages upon which such occasions play.

Each porch has its own persona. It may be a busy front porch with lots of coming and going, a private retreat complete with a cozy swing for two, or a simple farmhouse

ABOVE AND OPPOSITE: *With its Moroccan-style furnishings, this gallery overlooking a courtyard transports occupants to another world. Everything from the cushioned banquette to the color palette to the end tables with their star designs contributes to the exotic feel.*

porch with a string of laundry snapping across its comely front. Regardless of the particular style, each porch has the potential not only to live in harmony with the architecture of the house, but also to speak to both the changing of the seasons and the constant shifting of our moods and lives. Stations of tranquillity, porches help transport us from the mundane to the sublime.

Everything we do to further that sense of ease, that "this-is-the-life" feeling, will render our hours on the porch that much more enjoyable. And making a porch appealing, and above all comfortable, is relatively simple. Think about how you will use the porch and who will be using it with you. Putting together an outdoor room is similar to designing an indoor one. Furniture, fabrics, color, accessories, and balance all come into play when trying to create a space that is both serviceable and beautiful. What makes the decorating of a porch unique is the fact that you have the world at your doorstep; flowers, clouds, trees, and sunlight are all there, ready and waiting. Let these natural components, these unbeatable show-stoppers, be your real inspiration, and have fun. A porch can be as casual or as formal as you want—the tone is up to you. As with gardening, playing with the setting, perfecting it, editing out the superfluous, and introducing fresh touches are all factors of the unending pleasure.

Keep in mind that a porch these days is more than a place to be passed through on the way into the house. It can serve as a quiet spot for such simple activities as bird-

watching and stargazing, a glorious dining room for sharing sumptuous alfresco meals, or a luxurious retreat complete with a soothing hot tub for the ultimate in relaxation. Glean ideas that will work for you from the following chapters, and then add your own spin. Your personal stamp is what will make the difference between an ordinary porch and a cherished haven.

# CHAPTER ONE

# Timeless Appeal

ABOVE: *Designed as an entry, the Porch of the Maidens offers a graceful transition from the heat of the blazing sun to the temple's cool interior.*

OPPOSITE: *The rocker-lined porch of a Gothic cottage invites lingering. White gingerbread trim is like icing on a cake.*

THE PORCH LOOMS LARGE IN OUR COLLECTIVE MEMORY, AS NEARLY every culture has had porches. The Greeks can lay claim to one of the most famous and striking of all. Poised on the northern side of the Acropolis in Athens, the Erechtheum—a temple named for a legendary king—boasts the Porch of the Maidens. This portico features six graceful eight-foot [2.4m] -tall sculptured females (caryatids) that are employed architecturally. Their slender draped figures, each having one knee slightly bent, are the supporting columns, and their ornate headdresses form the capitals. Arranged in perfect symmetry, these dramatic forms epitomize the classical style. Ancient porches such as this served as formal entrances.

Roman temples had porticoes, too. Think of the Pantheon, rebuilt between 117 and 128 A.D. by the Roman emperor Hadrian. One of the most illustrious buildings in the world, the Pantheon was designed with a rectangular colonnaded porch. Almost every early Roman town, in fact, had one temple or more, and each had a portico. In Istanbul, the renowned fourteenth-century temple known as the Kariye Djami has both outer and inner porches decorated with extraordinary mosaics. And four centuries later, on the other side of the Atlantic, when George Washington built his beloved Mount Vernon on the banks of the Potomac River in Virginia, he included a soaring two-story porch overlooking the water.

Porches, it seems, are a universal phenomenon. Intent on creating a bridge between indoors and out, humankind has included porches of some sort or another

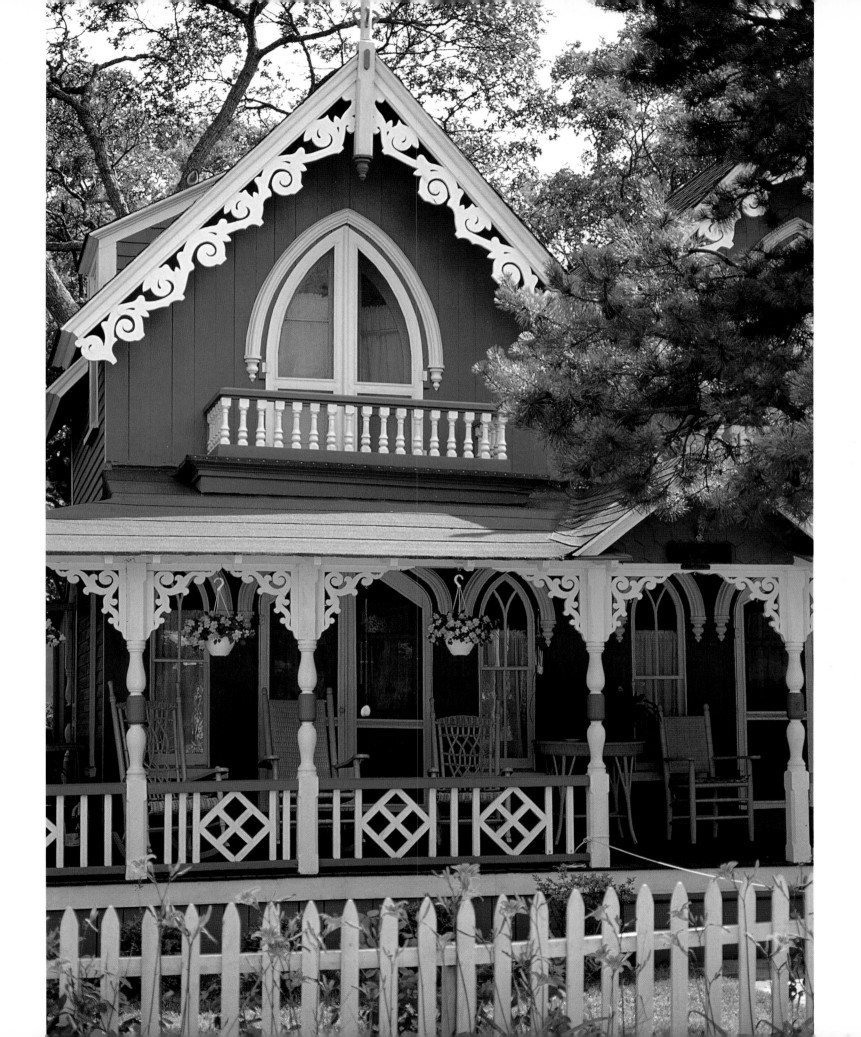

BELOW: *The stone-floored porch of an island house affords shade to twin lounge chairs and shelter from tropical afternoon showers. Just watching the breeze rattle the spiky palm fronds is relaxing. Should a rainbow surface, the owners have the best seats in the house.*

on all different types of buildings: Japanese Shinto shrines, villas in the Italian countryside, boxy modern abodes on the California coastline. Whatever we label these architectural features—loggias, galleries, verandas, porticoes, or breezeways—the bountiful enjoyment they afford us remains the same. Structured for group gatherings as well as solitary pursuits, the porch becomes much more than just a transition space. And it is as much about dreams as it is about reality.

## Porch Styles

Influenced originally by the country of origin, architectural styles metamorphose and overlap. The farther they travel from their source in both distance and time, the more apt they are to be altered. The skill of the builders and designers, the traditions drawn upon, and the availability of materials (from timber, stone, and brick to steel, plywood, and cement) have all resulted in innovations. And porches are not at all immune to these structural types of changes. Adaptable, personable, and practical, porches are, in fact, architectural chameleons. We have built them in hundreds of different guises, and though some may be more nondescript than others, they never disappoint. Wherever climate permits, we have thrown open the doors and embraced the outside world—while maintaining the comforts of home.

ABOVE: *Greek Revival architectural forms and ornamentation turn up on houses in nearly every region. Here, amid the palm trees, a stunning columned portico offers shade and shelter. To update the classical facade, the owners added an iron railing and masses of fragrant shrubs.*

Porches are found grafted onto homes in all sorts of styles, from Queen Anne to Spanish Colonial to Stick. Construction usually takes one of two basic forms: the porch is either set under the main roof of the house as an inset, or it is an independent agent with its own roof. Columns or posts may be employed as supports, and there is often some sort of low wall or railing.

An Adamesque home may have a small entrylike porch, while a Gothic Revival will sport a grand front porch with elaborate gingerbread trim. A rustic log cabin is likely to have a porch of rough-hewn boards and a railing of uneven, crisscrossed timbers; at the other end of the spectrum, a porch on a pitch-roofed manor house nestled in the French countryside will include a handsome balustrade.

Naturally, such details as the shape of the spindles in the railing or the form and material of the columns heighten a porch's personality and help us to recognize its genealogy. For instance, the porch of a Craftsman bungalow typically has piers of rock, while a modernist abode may have a cool horizontal balustrade. But porches have frequently been altered and added on to according to the wishes of their owners.

OPPOSITE: *Soaring Corinthian columns, characterized by fluted shafts and elaborate acanthus-leaf capitals, impart an air of grandeur to a house that borrows much from the architecture of ancient Greece. Classical details combine with elements from much later eras, including stained glass door insets, cast-iorn railings, and intricate grille-work.*

ABOVE: *Southern-style porches have always been designed to beat the heat. Wraparound galleries allow breezes to sweep through upstairs rooms as well as downstairs ones. Here, an elaborate double-sided staircase gives visitors and family alike the opportunity to make a grand entrance.*

LEFT: *A closer look reveals the elaborate detailing of this stunning porch. A classic dentiled cornice highlights the striking Corinthian columns guarding the front door. Thanks to a deft use of color, the architectural embellishments become more pronounced.*

OPPOSITE: *A porch with a curve as sensuous as a seashell looks crisp and pretty all summer long with a blue and white decor. The azure ceiling, according to folklore, will deter pesky bugs. Regardless of tradition, though, the peaceful blue ceiling simply causes the classic white wicker furniture beneath to shine. Various seats offer opportunities for socializing as well as quiet moments for reading. Seasonal flowers step up the festive air.*

BELOW: *The use of natural materials is a hallmark of the Craftsman-style bungalow. Here, hefty stone piers support the roof structure. Built close to the ground, this sort of porch encourages communication with nature. Against the stone backdrop, a rustic bench looks right at home.*

Latticework, scrollwork, unique braces and trusses, windows and doors are all possible additions for dressing up a porch or simply transforming its first intent. On an old porch, telling details such as cornices may help determine an approximate date of construction, but porches, like some people, are not always forthcoming about age. And many new porches are a congenial medley of various styles that have been cleverly reinterpreted and blended.

In the end, it's primarily location (urban or pastoral, East or West) and climate that continue to influence design and construction. A contemporary home overlooking a beautiful lake requires only a minimally adorned porch devoid of railings and plantings that might actually hinder the picture. Meanwhile, an urban porch calls out for a closed railing that will ensure greater privacy. One porch may demand a wall of lattice to ward off the blazing sun, while another may open like a wildflower to harvest the mountain breeze.

Porch decoration? Well, that takes its cue from all kinds of sources—from history, design trends, the talents of its owners (decorative painting, woodworking), even regional idiosyncrasies. It's not uncommon to find seaside houses with a compass

rose painted on the porch floor. A circle divided into thirty-two points, this old-world emblem is a mariner's tool, similar to a compass, for determining direction. What better ornament for a salt-sprayed cottage? Moving away from the coast into farm country, we're more apt to find ceilings that have been gussied up with a coat of robin's-egg blue. Farmers have claimed for centuries that this heavenly paint color shoos away pesky bugs and soothes the people who gather below. The hue certainly imbues the porch setting with celestial overtones, charmingly blurring the boundaries between inside and out even further. The wood floor may be the dull gray of a Navy battleship but overhead, every day is fair.

We all know an iron horseshoe nailed over the door, ends up, is said to bring good luck. In some areas, a wooden or plastic owl posted on a window shutter is thought to prevent birds from building

# PORCH PRIMER

PORCHES, BOTH OLD AND NEW, COME IN ALL SORTS OF SHAPES AND STYLES AND HAVE ALL SORTS OF COMPONENTS AND embellishments. Like bonnets on parade, some are more outlandish than others. While some are indeed quite modest, more than a few attain belle-of-the-ball status. Here's a sampling of architectural terms to help you distinguish between the different elements of porch design:

**Balustrade:** A series of balusters (small vertical members) connected by a rail at the top and bottom.

**Belvedere:** A gazebolike struture attached to a porch or, on occasion, a roof.

**Board-and-batten:** A siding that is constructed from vertical boards; the joints are covered by narrow wood strips referred to as battens. This type of siding is often seen on Gothic-style porches.

**Cornice:** The projecting finish at the top of a porch.

**Eaves:** The part of the roof, supported by rafters or brackets, that overhangs the wall and, as a result, provides shade below.

**Gingerbread:** A fanciful and intricate turned or sawed wood-work embellishment. This elaborate type of ornamentation frequently turns up on Gothic and Queen Anne houses, among others.

**Loggia:** An open-sided gallery, usually lined with pillars. It can appear on a first floor or an upper story.

**Pediment:** A low-pitched triangular feature over a doorway or a small porch. Reminiscent of a classical facade, a pediment often appears on Greek Revival–style homes.

**Pier:** An upright masonry structure supporting an upper floor or roof. Frank Lloyd Wright's Prairie-style homes sport massive, handsome, come-lean-against-me piers.

**Pilaster:** A flattened column attached to a wall and projecting slightly from it for decoration. Georgian houses sometimes display these along their facades.

**Portico:** A porch, usually used as an entry, framed by columns and topped off with a pediment. Although a classic feature, a portico is often grafted onto modern buildings such as ranch houses, too. Disconcerting as that mixture of styles might sound, a portico can soften a ranch's exterior in much the same manner that a silk scarf flatters an unembellished neckline.

**Truss:** A group of structural members arranged and fastened in a triangular unit to form a framework for the porch roof. Porches of Stick-style houses often have trusses as well as diagonal or curving brackets.

**Veranda:** Typically, a large porch rambling around two or more sides of a house. A top-of-the-list staging area for a large party on a summer evening.

their nests on a porch. A sprig of pungent rosemary, hung like mistletoe, is said to promote fond memories and bind friendships. And lilacs are said to impart both happiness and health. Old superstitions, every one, but they are sweet nonetheless. Porches accept such flights of fancy, maybe even encourage them. Take off your watch, let down your hair, and dare to be idle, these seasoned temptresses whisper. Who are we to disobey?

Whatever the shape, size, style, or embellishments, porches always come across as enticing and familiar. No matter how many photographs we study or how many residential streets we explore, we sense the similarity. Each and every one is a place where we could kick off our shoes and feel at home. The snug porch of a flower-filled Arts and Crafts–era bungalow—shaded on a hot summer's day by its low-pitched roof—is as charming to us as the airy gazebo tucked at the elbow of a rambling Victorian porch. What draws us, speaks to our senses, and impels us to want to stop the car and actually climb the steps is the welcome we anticipate. Safe, cool, and quiet, every porch extends an invitation to linger.

ABOVE: *A whimsical Victorian-style porch filled with wicker furniture offers endless possibilities. Whether used as a seating area or for dining, the gazebolike feature entices us to stay for a while. On all sides, nature is the show.*

## The Renaissance

As our days grow increasingly hectic, filled with the demands of the workplace and the race to keep up with technology, porches are becoming more important as places where we can unwind. Having to spend so much of our time inside, sitting in the midst of artificial lighting and often windowless surroundings, we crave greater exposure to the outdoors. Most of us need a natural and spiritual antidote to our high-stress world. And with their usual array of comfortable seats and swings, hammocks and pillows, porches are friendly spaces that reach out to people of all ages. Our parents knew this,

RIGHT AND BELOW: *Stretching the length of the house, an expansive porch accommodates big gatherings of family and friends who long for whole days spent outdoors. Different levels not only allow for different activities, but also help to break down the large space into more intimate settings. The lower level, for instance, is furnished to foster quiet conversation. Iced tea in the afternoon melts into evening cocktails. As the sun goes down, the lights go on and nobody considers leaving.*

and their parents before them. From dawn until dusk, in sun or moonlight, in rain (and how memorable is the patter of rain on a porch roof!) or fair weather, we can come together with friends and family and find solace in one another's company. Or we can sit on the porch by ourselves and rejoice in quiet reflection. Whether we're in this outdoor setting for a few moments or a few hours, we feel instantly lighter and substantially refreshed. A brand-new rising sun or the zigzagging flight of a monarch butterfly is all the amusement required after a busy week.

When it comes to more spacious Victorian or contemporary homes where the porch sometimes swirls around three sides, lucky owners can follow the path of the planets, timing their rituals to catch nature's best shows: breakfast on the east side with the children, cocktails on the west side with guests. But in the end, it's not just a grand design that compels us to linger in a rocker or to camp out on a swing. On a handkerchief-size porch, an old-fashioned glider cooled by a creaky overhead fan will evoke a simpler but equally romantic ambience. And the teeniest urban back-yard, seen from a wicker armchair, can seem a personal Garden of Eden.

BELOW: *Although snug, this suburban front porch is no less enticing than its larger counterparts. A porch swing and a few hanging baskets of red blooms are all it takes to bathe occupants in a calm, peaceful feeling.*

LEFT: *Along an uncrowded stretch of coastline, an illusion of shelter is enough to kindle a sense of privacy. The openness of the architecture creates numerous windows to the sea and sky, allowing porch-goers to soak up the wonder of a day at the beach.*

BELOW: *A mountain locale calls for a rustic log cabin and, in turn, a porch as comfortable as a pair of favorite work boots. The hefty timbers imbue the setting with a sense of solidity. But the porch's true beauty lies in its simplicity.*

Each porch is a celebration of life beyond the confines of fixed walls, a connection to the superior scheme of seasons and seeds. Out on the porch, away from the usual distractions and pressures, we are at once sheltered and liberated. And out of such ease, fresh thoughts emerge and traditions are born. Not that long ago, storytelling was a fine-tuned porch art. Transcending even cultural barriers, stories—family stories and fictional stories—were passed from porch to porch. Many of the tales recounted on those balmy nights have woven themselves like summer vines into literature, and they endure in spite of movies and television. William Faulkner wrote of soft evenings on porches, of hushed voices and fireflies. Indeed, the inventory of

writers who have mused about their porch memories—such as Thomas Wolfe, Mark Twain, Eudora Welty, and Pat Conroy—could fill a book.

Today's architects and builders recognize that porches throughout the ages have served a variety of important functions—both ecological and social. In some planned communities, sidewalks and front porches are now mandated in order to help families connect to one another—to foster that traditional experience of gathering together and sharing lives. People out for a walk with a stroller or a dog greet neighbors sitting on a porch, and relationships begin, some of which will last a lifetime. The ubiquitous wooden rockers may be replaced by aluminum numbers in such heart-stopping colors as tomato red and brilliant blue, the sleek tables may be sand-blasted glass, and the porch railings iron, but the appealing, livable aura of these outdoor rooms continues to be a happy discovery for each new generation.

Our love affair with porches comes as no surprise. We only need to open the door and go out on the porch to relax—no travel arrangements, no reservations (except staking claim to a favorite seat), no extra expenses. On the other side of the door is an instant vacation. Without a porch, however, we're more likely to remain inside, isolated from our communities to a great extent and missing out on the natural treasures that surround us every day: clouds and trees, rays of sunlight, grapes swelling on an arbor, or a flock of noisy geese heading south.

Porches are blank canvases to be shaped into whatever suits us best. They can easily be rendered more open or more private, more attuned to a favorite activity such as bird-watching or watercolor painting, or simply more restful—more suited to a grandmother with a story to tell and a child in her lap who wants to listen. We've finally come to understand that porches, timeless and forever rewarding, may be the very best and sweetest slice of home life.

OPPOSITE: *Along the front porch of a summer cottage, cushioned rockers line up in anticipation of many leisurely hours. The friendly setup lets occupants chat with passersby, while the dazzling architectural trim bids neighbors to slow down and visit for a bit.*

ABOVE: *What better way to encourage gathering, conversation, and storytelling than by including a fireplace on the porch. The mesmerizing flames draw friends and family, provide natural illumination as nighttime approaches, and extend the use of the porch into the colder months. Notice how two distinct chair styles vie for attention. While one fits in with the contemporary architecture, the other speaks to the natural surroundings.*

## CHAPTER TWO

# Sitting a Spell

*ABOVE: A burnished wood floor and soft yellow walls give this front porch a friendly demeanor, while a decorative wreath issues a warm welcome.*

*OPPOSITE: Outfitted with plenty of tables and seating, this porch functions as an outdoor living room that can be enjoyed both day and night.*

USPENDED MIRACULOUSLY BETWEEN THE OUTDOOR WORLD AND the indoor one, porches are amicable rooms that only improve the more they are lived in and relished. The sweater left on the back of the chair, the three sets of sneakers eased off and now parked beneath the table—these are tokens of just how relaxed we can be here. From early morning to late at night, a porch affords us protection from the elements and unbound pleasure. We can chart the comings and goings of the birds, or simply close our eyes, listen to their song, and drift. Years from now, we'll hear the bang of a screen door and be reminded of a great many happy occasions with a porch at the heart of them all.

Every day, thousands of us collect our morning newspaper from the front porch steps, and before the rest of the world stirs, we claim a hushed few minutes for ourselves. But despite these moments of peace, porches love crowds: families gathering on a lazy Sunday afternoon, friends sharing recipes, neighbors hashing over the local gossip. We add a chair or two, station a footstool by a rocker, throw an extra cushion on a vintage glider. The more comforts we pile on, the more welcoming the porch becomes.

There are no rigid rules or unforgiving furnishings on the porch. A space destined to be enjoyed through months of blossoms and vivid leaf turnings demands that we veto the splintery bench and the uptight slipcover that won't wash well. Instead, to foster these moments of kicking back and talking, we want feel-good furnishings that encourage whiling away the hours in their embrace. We want to coax people to put their feet up and stretch out. We want the sort of comfort that we get from our favorite pair of blue jeans, and nothing less will do.

# Setting the Stage

When we collect our friends and family around us, we want them to be as content and at ease as we are when we sit alone savoring that early moment of solitude. How we situate the furniture, of course, will have a great deal to do with making our time, and theirs, more pleasurable. First, we'll want to take advantage of the attributes of the setting—after all, the setting is a big part of what draws us out to the porch to begin with. If there are yachts nestled in the harbor, we'll want to pull our chairs closer for a view. If there's a grassy expanse with tree-filled mountain ridges in the distance, we'll want to be poised to best appreciate this spectacular vista. In an urban setting, we're more likely to focus our attention toward the house. However, the forms of many standard porches—long and thin, or boxlike—do present their decorating challenges.

## MAKING THE ARRANGEMENTS

One key to an inviting porch is to establish individual islands of intimacy. On a long, thin porch, designate two tables, for instance, as anchoring centerpieces. Create one sitting arrangement with a love seat and two ample armchairs positioned around a low

RIGHT: *Inviting rocking chairs are positioned so that occupants can sit back, take in the breathtaking waterfront view, and monitor the comings and goings of the boats. The use of simple white furnishings keeps all the attention focused on the enchanting natural scenery.*

OPPOSITE: *Even a compact porch can play host to different activities simultaneously. Here, a table and matching chairs fashion a convenient spot for enjoying meals or working on craft projects, while a pair of chunky rockers invite reading, chatting, and just plain resting. One person can linger over a salad while another dozes— no compromising necessary.*

RIGHT: *On this narrow front porch, a table and a pair of chairs are turned on the diagonal to work with the architecture of the house. An area rug follows suit, lending definition to the cozy sitting area. With a place for resting drinks and seating made comfortable by plump pillows, the setup is both practical and congenial.*

coffee table—a setup that's perfect for smooth-flowing conversation, snacks, and even games. Forge another grouping with a large round table—well suited to dining—and a group of Windsor-style chairs in steel, wood, or plastic. According to the principles of *feng shui*, the ancient Chinese art of placement, tables are not only functional, but also help people feel that they share a common bond. To establish a sense of balance, both seating arrangements should carry approximately the same visual weight. Rugs—sisal, sea grass, or cotton—laid beneath the furniture will help define boundaries and make each grouping seem cordial. Sisal and straw rugs without padding, which tends to hold moisture, will endure a summer on the porch as long as they are protected from rain. Cotton rugs are more susceptible to mildew and are best used in dry climates. To defy storms, a floorcloth—painted and sealed—is ideal.

Turning furniture on the diagonal also skillfully alters the feeling of a long, thin porch while bringing people together. By stationing a sofa or settee in this manner, you might create room for an extra chair or two at either end of the structure. If space allows, a sofa might also be set crossways—rather than against a wall—to help visually expand the porch. Sly moves such as these appear to increase square footage. Highlight curves or angles with rugs laid on the diagonal as well. If you paint the short sides of a skinny porch a warm color and the longer sides in a light shade, your outdoor room will seem less like a tunnel.

Paint can also be used to open up a compact, boxlike porch. A pale hue will visually enlarge the space and infuse it with a lighthearted quality. Furnishings with an airy look, such as those made of wrought-iron or wicker, will have a similar effect. To soften the harsh angles of the box-shaped porch, position chairs on an angle in the corners. As you arrange the furnishings, be sure to keep a path clear for people entering and leaving the house.

Expansive front porches—where the furniture appears to stretch off into the distance or vanish around a corner—are wonderful for parties, when everybody is on their feet, but less wonderful when it comes to quiet conversation. Experts have determined that a distance of greater than eight feet (2.4m) between people makes talking a struggle tantamount to running up a hill with a heavy backpack. You certainly don't want friends hollering or craning to catch a word. Feng shui practitioners believe that such a distressing abyss also leads to bad *ch'i*, or unwelcome cosmic energy, resulting in discord. It is better to have several small seating areas, which will remedy the situation and promote engaging discussions no matter how large the guest list grows.

### LIGHTWEIGHT, WILL TRAVEL

By envisioning friends coming together and by taking note of how they place themselves when they are on your porch, you can better map out where a chair or a table should be positioned. One corner may be perfect in the late afternoon for settling in to work on a crossword puzzle, but far too hot at noon. Be forewarned: pieces on the porch are often on the move anyway. Less reticent to rearrange things on a porch than they would be inside the living

BELOW: *White wicker chairs placed on an angle transform this tiny front porch into a peaceful outdoor sitting area. Situated on either side of the door, the chairs provide comfortable resting spots without interfering with the flow of traffic.*

RIGHT: *In this tantalizing spot, the furnishings are far enough apart to provide plenty of legroom for everyone, but close enough so that friends and family can chat without straining to hear one another. Should occupants wish to edge their chairs closer for a private tête-à-tête, they can do so quite effortlessly, thanks to the easy-to-lift wicker pieces. Wearing the same paint color, the wicker furnishings form a cohesive and attractive union. A painted white iron and glass table provides a refreshing counterpoint.*

OPPOSITE, TOP: *Echoing the curves of the architecture, a round table becomes the centerpiece of a formal porch. From flouncy, shade-providing drapes to painted floorboards, the carefully contrived scene is all about details.*

OPPOSITE, BOTTOM: *A closer look at the table reveals that it is far from your basic piece of furniture. The game that appears to be in progress is actually a trompe l'oeil design (only the pistachios and one deck of cards are real). The dealt cards, the score pad, and even the plate of cheese and crackers are painted on the surface.*

PAGE 36: *Wicker chairs gang up in separate areas to allow several different conversations to take place at once. Easily turned to one side or another, though, the chairs can be shifted to bring everyone into one discussion. A small, lightweight table goes wherever it's needed.*

PAGE 37: *Two unusual tables do more than hold magazines and snacks; they add to the exotic ambience of the space. The star-shaped example has been hand-painted in a pattern that pays homage to Islamic art, while the side table is ornamented more simply with a double-scalloped edge.*

room, guests will often shift a table or a chair so that it is more to their liking without giving it a second thought. Over comes a stool to prop up someone's sunburned feet, there goes a chair closer to the steps so someone can supervise a group of children playing in the grass beyond.

That said, when picking out furnishings consider mobility. Doing so will not only prevent guests from getting hurt when they take it upon themselves to rearrange your porch, but it will also give you the flexibility to move pieces around to better accommodate different numbers of people or different activities. Cast-iron chairs may be stunning, but they're a nuisance to lug about. In fact, they're real home wreckers when dragged across a floor. A better choice would be lightweight aluminum or wicker furniture. If you live near the ocean, make sure that the aluminum has been suitably

treated to resist salt-air corrosion, and remember to bring the pieces indoors when a fierce wind threatens. And in all settings, any wicker you use should be the weather-proofed variety. Reserve antique wicker for indoor use.

## FURNISHINGS FOR LIVING

Ideally, a porch will have a number of tables. Often labeled occasional tables, these workhorses perform all sorts of duties. There might be one for card playing, one for letter writing, and one for the massive ongoing jigsaw puzzle that surfaces every summer and is never brought to fruition. Small bunches of fresh flowers plucked from the garden will make each of these surfaces an outpost of welcome. If tight quarters forbid such extravagance, incorporate one long table that affords room for sailors to spread out charts or—with the addition of a tablecloth and a few extra chairs—relatives to stay for an impromptu supper after an early evening swim.

A collection of rocking chairs will also be appreciated. Creak and groan, back and forth, the wobbly sound of rockers on a porch is an age-old lullaby that calms us.

ABOVE: *Oversize wicker furniture does more than pump up the comfort level. Large as they may be, such pieces remain airy in construction. Similarly, glass-top tables, though substantial in size, contribute a sense of openness and spaciousness that prevents the milieu from feeling heavy or oppressive.*

By setting chairs in a line, we make it easy for occupants to watch the world go by, or the sun go down, while they talk and rock. When we think of rockers, most of us conjure up visions of wooden chairs. But designers have successfully launched these gracious pieces of furniture into the future with a variety of materials, finishes, and colors. Old-fashioned-looking wicker rockers and all kinds of other assorted pieces are available today in special polypropylene resins that require zero maintenance no

matter how low the temperature plummets. Chair pads for these types of seats are generally made of weather- and mold-resistant acrylic and include a special drip-through construction that also defies moisture.

If your porch is on the small side, don't think that you're constrained to stunted furniture. Overscale pieces will give porches of a more modest size some stature and raise their luxury quotient. Chunky wooden rockers wearing thick cushions will look

ABOVE: *Defying the constraints of the architecture, big wicker chairs, complete with thick cushions, transform a narrow porch into a gracious and somewhat grand-looking outdoor living room. A slim wooden bench, pressed up against the wall of the house, allows room for a coffee table.*

BELOW: *A large porch accommodates several seating areas. Sofas drawn up around the hearth are natural roosting spots. In such a hospitable milieu, traditional-looking porch furniture can coexist effortlessly with pieces usually found indoors.*

more grounded and more inviting to visitors than twin colonial rockers with dainty woven seats.

Any porch can benefit from a slinky chaise for catnapping or a set of sleek wooden steamer chairs. Wicker, iron, rattan, polyester? The style of the porch—be it traditional or contemporary—can be a guide to making selections, but it needn't dictate. A porch, easygoing and open-minded, allows ample room for all sorts of furniture: flea-market finds, Adirondack chairs, twig benches. Be a creative chef, if you will, and add different ingredients to the pot. Older porches accumulate furniture, hand-me-downs, and indoor rejects that find new life when they're cast in outdoor light. Should the scene start to look somewhat disjointed, a coat of white or black paint over everything will minimize the confusion. Designer's secret? Mismatched pieces come together well when they share a common bond, such as a certain color or fabric. Paint, particularly oil-based, also protects wood and wicker furnishings, prolonging their lives.

While you needn't be rigidly tied to matching furnishings to the architectural style of your home, when the two do speak to one another, you can achieve a real sense of balance. For instance, wicker, a favorite of the Victorians, is especially fitting on the porch of a Victorian-era home. The furniture of Gustav Stickley, whose angular designs were a pared-down response to what he saw as Victorian excess, would probably be less well suited. Along similar lines, certain pieces will just look better on the

porch of an 1830s Greek Revival than a 1920s Spanish Revival. And modern porches often fare well when the furnishings are as streamlined as the construction; this way, the architecture itself—pure of line and of purpose—takes the spotlight. Beneath a new and shiny metal roof, a minimal-style pristine clapboard porch cringes at the thought of ruffles and stenciled window boxes. More to its liking? An anodized aluminum table with four matching, perforated chairs, which would be equally as beautiful and enticing standing alone on the front porch of a stucco-and-glass house. Keep in mind that subtle nuances in texture will play out here just as they do inside the home, often with surprising results. Natural elements—such as ceramic, wood, and stone—belong outdoors, where their tactile qualities can be appreciated in combination with one another. A simple drum-shaped earthenware garden seat (smooth), perhaps glazed the color of wet grass, can be juxtaposed with a pair of rattan chairs (textured) to form an appealing vignette. To add anything would be overdressing.

ABOVE: *Rugged Adirondack furniture suits the rustic nature of this mountain hideaway. In keeping with the unpainted ceiling above, the chair and table retain their natural color. Stone crocks can be filled with wildflowers or geraniums for an instant jolt of color.*

The real test? Sit in the chair, lie on the hammock, or sip a cold beverage at the table. If what you've chosen feels right to you, if your friends and family are enjoying themselves, then you know you have succeeded.

## Colorful Appeal

Every porch has its own topography. But as the natural light washing across it changes during the day, the face of the terrain changes, too. Morning sunbeams bring out the grain in a polished bare wood floor, while noon rays flatten it. Study the porch's layout the way you would a bedroom. Consider how much sun and shadow pass across the porch and whether you want to establish a feeling of coziness or airiness.

OPPOSITE: *At the hottest time of day, a pergola throws a shadow across a wraparound built-in bench. The pergola's honey-colored wood warms up the cool tones of the scene below. A construction such as this could be covered with a sweep of bougainvillea for a showy canopy.*

ABOVE: *Bold hues enliven a trio of simple Adirondack chairs. As bright as the flowers below, the seating arrangement dispels gloominess, even on the dreariest of days.*

Large trees and tall buildings sometimes throw a porch into deep shade, which although welcome on a stifling day, can make the space seem somewhat gloomy. Glum is a four-letter word in an outdoor space, so if this is the situation on your porch, consider incorporating some color to rev things up. Vibrant colors will make a porch seem more intimate, while cool tones will visually expand the boundaries. Take note of the color of the house's exterior walls: the soft, neutral, gray background of weathered shingles, for instance, makes a suitable foil for crisp blues and vivid greens, whether they appear in furniture frames or fabrics. A colonial home painted bright red like a valentine cries out for quieter choices—more subtle fittings that won't make a mockery of its cheerful disposition.

Look around, look up and down, and enlist the colors that catch your attention—the snappy yellow of a daffodil, the rosy hue of a robin's breast, the glossy green of a holly tree. There are all sorts of sources for inspiration. If there are mounds of blue hydrangeas billowing across the front of your porch, let that blue be your starting point and build from there. Or simply choose fabrics and accessories that match this breathtaking color, add some white furniture, and announce the resulting color combination as your theme. Blue and white, a never-failing fit as endearing as nineteenth-century Canton porcelain china, is a time-honored color pairing.

ABOVE: *As charming in a porch setting as it is on fine china, the combination of blue and white never fails to please. Here, the duo appears not only on the furnishings but on the architecture as well.*

## Stylish Threads

When selecting fabric coverings and cushions for furnishings, there are a number of considerations to take into account. You'll want to choose fabrics that are not only visually appealing, but comfortable and durable as well.

Popular fabrics—ones that have been around for years and remain appropriate for a well lived-on porch—run the gamut from faded chintz to ticking in blue, black, or red. New synthetic fabrics that resist dampness and mildew include acrylics that have the look and feel of cotton, vinyl-coated polyester (also used for table umbrellas), and laminated cotton. Acrylics designed for outdoor use are usually UV-resistant, which means that the colors won't fade as quickly from the sun's rays. Those acrylics that are "solution-dyed" will last the longest.

Masters of the quick change, slipcovers can update and transform any ho-hum seat, from straight-backed dining chairs to comfy sofas. Almost too good to be true, they offer the ultimate in flexibility. If you are going the slipcover route, choose fabrics such as cotton or denim that can be laundered easily and will stand up to wet bathing suits and foggy nights (nights when you forget to bring the cushions inside). Slipcovers also come in the synthetic fabrics discussed above. Like party dresses, these means of disguise can be fussy or tailored. Leave off the ruffle at the bottom and a chair will show off its legs for a cleaner, fresher look.

In the worry-free environment of a porch, there is nothing like the security that comes from knowing no harm will be done if the muddy dog curls up on the chair or a child spills some juice. On the porch, such incidents are part of the tapestry of living. And laundering slipcovers and pillow covers will not only get rid of spots, but will make the fabrics softer. Just remember to allow for some shrinkage, and don't worry about ironing. If wrinkles do concern you, put the clean slipcovers back on while they're still slightly damp, flattening out the creases with your hands. Larger, looser slipcovers are always rumpled—a trait that makes them endearing.

ABOVE: *Outside or in, floral patterns blend beautifully with plaid or checks. And when the colors are crisp and bright, the mood of the whole scene lifts. Less likely to show dirt or stains, these busy designs welcome kids and pets. To heighten interest—and comfort— extra pillows in different shapes and sizes line the old-fashioned swing.*

WHEN YOU DECORATE YOUR PORCH, PULL OUT ALL THE STOPS and let the world see the extent of your imagination, the depth of your creativity. While the traditional bunch of Indian corn and the green wreath over the knocker are not to be scoffed at, the celebration of a season and all its glory deserves a more powerful, take-notice statement. So when summer and all its frills fold, banish the delicate flowers and the warm-weather flags, and set your sights on the robust vegetables and the deck-the-hall fruits. Opt for not-so-subtle changes that will bring you full circle while continually holding you close to nature, which is, as always, the very best place to turn for inspiration.

In autumn, pay attention to the tones of the landscape—reds, oranges, golds, deep purples, bronze—and incorporate them into the porch setting. Off go the floral fabrics, on go rich, regal colors. If you don't want to replace slipcovers, simply layer on throws, blankets, and pillows in darker plaids and checks. And bring in the harvest: berries, rose hips, dried corn, wheat, pumpkins, and ornamental gourds in all their wonderful shapes, from curved-neck spoon gourds to green dippers to Turk's turbans. All of these farm-stand gleanings are perfect candidates. Pile them in the center of a table, or mound them in a large, low basket by the door, varying color and texture. If it's shiny gourds you want, spray them with clear acrylic or rub on wax or lemon oil. Tie a generous bunch of dried corn stalks, along with streamers of zesty bittersweet vine, to each porch pillar, or set out a friendly jack-o'-lantern on each porch step. For a party, shun the everyday coffee table and enlist a bale of hay to play the part. By late autumn, the bugs are long gone, so plug in a table lamp (perhaps one with a paper shade decorated with a bat cut from black paper)

and forge a pool of light that can glow like a candle when the trick-or-treaters arrive.

Come the winter holidays, drape garlands of pungent greens along the railings and around the posts, mass terra-cotta pots and tin cachepots holding small evergreens of varying sizes by the door (the trees can be planted in the yard when the ground thaws), and collect heaps of pinecones and rose-colored pomegranates to fill shiny galvanized buckets. Miniature white lights—strung everywhere—will transform the scene. And so will jaunty red bows. Buy or make small evergreen wreaths, tie them with the snazzy bows, and wire on whole fistfuls of faux red berries (no one will guess). Suspend the wreaths on wide ribbons in front of the windows and doors that face out to the porch. As a sign of your hospitality, post a portly pineapple over the door or in the middle of your biggest, greenest wreath.

For spring, bulbs will be the show. Plan on filling an assortment of fairly shallow containers in the autumn or winter. If yours is a warm climate, be sure the bulbs have been precooled. Moisten the soil, and set the containers in a protected place where they won't freeze. About once a month, give them some water, and at the first appearance of any green shoots—which should be just about when the weather starts warming up—you can scoot the flowers onto the porch. Be lavish: stuff window boxes, tubs, or perhaps something unexpected such as a low paint-washed concrete bowl. With forethought, you can have daffodils, narcissi, and tulips only weeks after the holiday decorations have been packed away. When the blooms die, remove the bulbs to be planted in the garden and fill up the empty spots with annuals. Or underplant the bulbs with cool-weather-loving flowers such as violas, pansies, and sweet alyssum, which will hide any fading foliage. On the front door, a May basket—a historical harbinger of a new solstice—overflowing with large pansies is a giddy note marking winter's end. A basket of forsythia will also present a cheerful greeting. If you don't have your own forsythia bush, beg some blooming branches from a friend. Gather these bright yellow flowers into a bucket, and place the arrangement where it will catch the sun.

With the return of summer, there is little need for decoration as nature provides a vast array of visual delights. However, for those who do desire something extra, floral adornments are certainly easy to come by. Raid your garden several times a week for fresh flowers or vines, and sprinkle these spontaneous arrangements on occasional tables throughout the porch. Fill an ironstone pitcher with wildflowers, an old apothecary jar with roses, or a dented tin pail with daylilies. A stand of gladioli by the door will lift the psyche. Feel free to make the most of the season's opulence—there are, after all, no rules.

OPPOSITE: *A rural porch comes alive at the holidays, thanks to fresh garlands of greenery winding their way around hefty pillars. But the festive spirit doesn't stop there; at the door, a lush wreath greets visitors. Simple but dramatic, these all-natural decorations work well with the rustic architecture.*

ABOVE: *Adapting to the season, this porch makes the most of the autumn harvest. An array of pumpkins and a basket filled with ornamental squash team up with colorful flowers to great success. A dried wreath adds to the effect, as do the stray leaves that blow in with the afternoon breeze.*

In lieu of a slipcover, a large piece of canvas or fabric can simply be thrown over a settee or chair and allowed to drape and fall as it will. For something a little more trim and tidy, the same length of fabric, a colorful quilt, or even a soft blanket can be draped and then pulled together at the corners and nonchalantly knotted. If you're renting a vacation house, these unrestrained and simple porch furniture covers will provide instant gratification minus any long-term investment, allowing you to put your own personal stamp on the place. Toss a swath of artist's canvas over a worn love seat, stack on the colored pillows, and voilà—Elysium.

Exposed to the sun, many fabrics quickly fade to pale imitations of their former glory. While some homeowners may opt to use UV-resistant synthetics for their prolonged vibrancy, others actually relish the muted look that comes from fading. A patina born of age or weather speaks of many good times, many good memories. And soft pastels are reminiscent of some of our best-loved summer flowers. If you want to hurry the fading process along, wash your pillow covers and slipcovers and then lay them out in direct sun to dry. In England and Ireland, linens are often thrown haphazardly—or so it looks—atop garden shrubs and bushes. The robust plantings, stiff as drying racks, allow air to circulate at the top and bottom.

BELOW: *Romantic wicker furniture welcomes creativity. Here, a happy gardener has combined a favorite ivy pattern with a whimsical design that includes a treasured phrase. A swath of rosy cloth covers the seat cushions.*

Wide, bright cabana stripes in black or dark green and white are classic choices for porch furnishings. But so, too, are any number of florals that mimic the blooms in bed and border. Bolder, busier patterns hide dirt (a plus for city porches), while jewel tones add zing. And checks, like those associated with gingham, are an all-time country winner. For balance, sprinkle the bolder patterns up and down the porch rather than clumping all the fireworks in one spot.

Take poetic license: combine patterns, checks, and stripes. Pillow covers needn't be copycats. But for continuity, keep all the patterns in the same color range and don't permit one pattern to overwhelm the others. Tie-on cushions make wooden or iron seats more comfortable for long stretches of sitting and, once again, different designs can function as a collaboration. Try a striped pattern for the cushions and polka dots for the ties. Decorative bindings, cords, fringe, and buttons marry well with porch pillows and, like the cherry atop a sundae, provide a thoughtful finishing touch. Plump up the cushions with a good thump so that sitters feel happily ensconced each time they perch. Remember, large pillows can also do double duty as seats on the floor.

## Savvy Strategies

Any accoutrements that can play a dual role will render the porch more hospitable for both large and small groups. Roly-poly ottomans are perfect examples—one day they're called into action as tables, the next day they're performing as seats. Collapsible deck chairs and small folding X-frame stools with colorful canvas seats are always good to have on hand and can easily be stacked out of the way when not in use. Scattered around a porch, small folding stools such as these—as well as folding wooden luggage stands topped with trays—can pose as tables. A tall folding stand with a sturdy tray top makes an attractive portable bar, too. Nesting tables are another good bet. Condensed, they keep a low profile as a single end table. Telescoped out to show off their graduated sizes, they can serve as innovative plant stands or hors d'oeuvre stations at a cocktail party. Pull them apart and they're off to wherever they're needed most.

People like to settle on porch railings and rest on porch steps. Make the latter even more appealing by adding a stenciled or rubber-stamped design. Or paint a graphic border to highlight the step's depth or width. For a charming country flair, paint the banisters and risers, and strip the treads to reveal the natural wood. A built-in seat—along the house wall,

BELOW: *When extra seating is called for, move in the director's chairs. Easily folded, such seats can be stashed in a closet when not in use. Notice how the one here ties in with the cheerful sunflowers stenciled on the walls. Birdhouses mounted on those same walls enhance the quirky charm of the space.*

ABOVE: *An appealing screened porch that's protected from the elements makes an ideal haven for reading or playing games.*

OPPOSITE: *A shiny tin pail holds croquet equipment, while a bench provides a prime spot for watching players on the lawn below.*

perhaps, or in a corner—can help to maximize seating on a smaller porch. Cap the seat with a comfy pad, and give it its own collection of fat pillows (square, rectangular, or round); the handy built-in will instantly become a pleasant nook for reading or resting. A big wicker basket filled with books and magazines is a must-have porch treat.

## Playtime and Peaceful Pursuits

You'll want to equip your outdoor living room with everything guests and family members might need to make the most of their time on the porch. For instance, you may want to have binoculars for bird-watching and a telescope for getting a closer look at passing sailboats or twinkling stars. Take the best telescope you can find, and post it at the end of the porch to be used by young and old alike. Small children often enjoy keeping a log of what they see—planets, large cruise ships on the distant horizon, a fiery red cardinal. Start a collection of binoculars, and place them next to sofas and

## STARSTRUCK

GAZING UP AT THE SKY FROM THE COMFORT OF A PORCH ON a summer night, we can potentially see some four thousand stars—without a telescope. In fact, constellations are best enjoyed with the naked eye. Because the earth rotates once every twenty-four hours and orbits the sun once a year, the scene above changes according to the season and the time of night. The most opportune time to take up a watch is just around the new moon, since the sky is particularly dark at that point. Switch off the lights in the house to thicken the blackness, and with a small pocket flashlight, consult a star chart or a planisphere to help you map your way. Like learning to play the piano, practice will render this almighty spectacle more familiar.

On a summer night, three of the brightest, hottest show stealers will be Vega, the flashiest star in the constellation Lyra; Arcturus, in the constellation Boötes; and orange-red Antares (three hundred times the diameter of the sun), in the constellation Scorpio. If it's dark enough, you might also see the Milky Way flung across the blackness. This is the galaxy that contains our solar system, a dazzling band of 100,000 million stars and

nebulae, twinkling balls of hydrogen and helium with nuclear fusion reactions occurring right in their steaming cores.

Everyone's favorite, the North Star—the most useful of all and the one we should point out to young children—can be located by finding the Big Dipper. The two stars farthest away from the Big Dipper's handle are the pointer stars pointing toward the North Star, which the ancient Chinese referred to as the Great Imperial Ruler of Heaven. Keep this one star in mind, and you won't lose your way.

Next to the sun and the moon, rocky-surfaced Venus is the brightest object in the sky. Roughly 7,516 miles (12,093km) in diameter (about the size of the earth), Venus is the second planet from the sun, though it is poetically referred to as a star. Lovers should look for it in the west right after sunset (the Evening Star) or in the east just before sunrise (the Morning Star).

Shooting stars are really meteors, small chunks of iron and nickel or broken comet bits. They hurl through the night sky, almost faster than we can track them, burn, and disappear. Look for them after midnight and before sunrise. And don't forget to make a wish—these "stars," after all, are said to be magic.

chairs (along with assorted field guides) to encourage guests and other family members to watch the wildlife and identify the birds they don't recognize. Station a variety of squirrel-proof feeders around the yard to attract different species. A cedar-shingle dovecote crowning its very own post is almost as lovely as the creatures it will draw, and a stone birdbath hosting a swimming party of finches is worthy of a photograph. Being able to participate in such simple pastimes is a rich reward of life on the porch.

Nature will play her hand—long afternoons of thunder and rain, a whole week of steady drizzle—but an assortment of games (checkers, backgammon, and Monopoly) and art supplies should provide satisfying diversions. A roll of white butcher paper is an instant canvas for children. Tear off a large piece of paper, tape it down over a table or on the floor, and let the kids be inspired by the natural world around them. A wooden or wicker chest makes a perfect home for crayons, chess boards, and anything else that kids (and adults) need to while away the hours. An inexpensive cabinet or armoire, enamel-painted to make it more durable, is also handy, and it brings the heft of a living room to the porch. If space allows, a child-size table-and-chair set will transform one corner of the porch into a special kids-only place. When not in use, the Lilliputian chairs can be hung on the wall on wooden pegs, Shaker style. Recruit a bookshelf for juvenile books only and maintain a toy basket, adding a stuffed animal, a doll, or a new truck every now and then to keep it fresh and interesting. When not in use, the basket can easily be slid beneath the skirt of a round table, ready for play at a moment's notice yet not underfoot. Toys and books that children can get into themselves are far more enticing than those that are doled out only upon request.

BELOW: *Portable stools are good game partners. Adults can reserve one for chess, while the kids claim others for reading materials and coloring. Drawing supplies and books can keep children content and occupied as the adults catch up with one another.*

## Lighting Up the Night

Across the way, the neighbors have turned on their lamps. Sitting out on the porch in the last translucent purple rays of a summer evening, though, we're reluctant to reach for even a candle. Hanging between the dark to come and the last glimmer of the day, we're savoring the changing colors of the sky. Misty layers of blue and orange lead to deep gray-blue, red, and purple, all of them seeming to hang one over another like chimney smoke. Sky watching is high on the list of porch pleasures and is practically a twenty-four-hour pastime. From early-morning shooting stars and fantastical cloud formations to big, splashy sunset finales and glittering constellations, the sky presents a perpetual show overhead.

To produce a different sort of light show on the porch, we turn to a dazzling host of options—everything from recessed lights and wall fixtures to chandeliers. By employing one or a combination, and by incorporating dimmers, it's possible to evoke an aura almost as restful—if not as amazing—as that created by nature. And lighting on the porch looks lovely when glimpsed from inside, especially when the source is

BELOW: *Arts and Crafts–style light fixtures that are in keeping with a bungalow's character grace this front porch, which also features classically styled columns. Mixing periods can be a successful way of enhancing a home's personality.*

a wrought-iron chandelier festooned with greens at holiday time. For safety, there should always be adequate illumination by steps and doorways and along paths leading to and from the porch. Subtle outdoor lighting that floods the spreading foliage of a beautiful tree or a carefully placed garden sculpture creates stunning accents to be enjoyed from the porch. Powered by their own superefficient cells, wireless solar lights will go on and off without being monitored. And strings of tiny electrical lights, in a variety of designs from fruits to seashells, can be looped around porch posts or draped like garlands along porch railings.

ABOVE: *On an expansive front porch, soft illumination is provided by unobtrusive fixtures sprinkled across the wall of the house. The lights not only serve occupants of the porch, but also act as friendly beacons for late-night arrivals. On cool evenings, the heartening glow of the outdoor fireplace is a romantic bonus.*

ABOVE: *Filled with tiny starlike lights, this festive display spreads holiday cheer to those inside and outside the home. Drape a sparkly garland along the porch railing and the whole neighborhood will sit up and take notice.*

OPPOSITE: *A jewel-tone pendant lamp suspended from the ceiling and a coordinating hurricane shade resting on the coffee table infuse this porch with an exotic flavor. Rattan furnishings suggest a tropical clime.*

Undoubtedly, though, candles lend themselves to porch life best. Possibilities include pillars nestled in stalwart glass hurricane shades; votives deposited in all kinds of glass, metal, or pottery containers; shiny metal-backed wall sconces; and tin lanterns and luminarias. Less harsh and more organic, candles are perfect partners for the outdoors. For a party, line the path up to the porch with a dozen luminarias, using humble white paper bags and sand to keep the votives (encased in their own glass containers) erect. Or opt for something a bit more formal but equally mesmerizing—perhaps a group of candle-burning Chinese temple lamps or an array of flame-burning tiki torches. Using the same sort of flame-inspired light both in the garden and on the porch makes for continuity and has a soothing effect on the eye, eliminating jarring adjustments from bright spots to dark. Furthermore, flickering light is said to draw people out and keep them more animated and alert.

To eliminate fuss, keep a tray full of votives on hand. That way, they can easily be toted in and out of the house or stashed away in a cupboard. To create a dramatic show, bring together an assortment of creamy white and beige candles—some slender, some thick and tall. The staggered array will delight the eye, while the candles' pale wax will appear all the more luminous in the dark. Light the whole bunch just as twilight descends to commemorate the end of the day. Or sprinkle them here and there like stars—on an end table, on the coffee table, in wall sconces—to form an earthbound galaxy. Wax drips (think of candles stuck in raffia-wrapped wine bottles) are part of the ceremony, as is a snuffer for extinguishing the flames.

Citronella candles—like coir-bristled welcome mats, flyswatters, and boot scrapers—are another example of useful porch fare. Today's market features such candles in numerous shapes and containers. Their scent, although pleasing to most, is powerful on a still night. It is best to line up these candles along the porch's perimeters instead of stationing them in the middle of the table, especially if you're serving food. For fun and for protection from bugs, tuck one fat citronella candle in something unexpected, like a jeweled Moroccan lamp, and suspend it where it's effective but not obtrusive. Citronella oil can also be used as an insect repellent. Fill a glass lamp, and let the pungent aroma waft gently through the air. A small fire extinguisher out of view but close at hand for an emergency is always a wise precaution when there are open flames.

## Enclosed Porches

As the world grows dark all around, we can soak up the night—all night if we choose—on a screened porch, safe and secure from the elements and the winged critters. Now is when the storytelling really starts to boil. Fueled by the lengthening shadows and the glow of candles on the faces of the people we hold dear, the porch becomes a mystical oasis. Laughter pierces the stillness of a summer evening and draws us even closer. Across streets and pastures, our voices carry, born aloft on the softest of breezes.

Reluctant to move inside for winter and leave this ethereal world behind, many homeowners replace their wire or plastic screens with glass panels. Such a shift—from screens to glass—extends a porch's life, at least for a few months. If there's a fireplace in the outdoor room—as is the case with many stone-floored porches—chilly nights become occasions for cooking on the hearth. What to serve to friends on an enclosed porch in late autumn? Scrumptious toasted marshmallows speared on long-handled skewers, hot chocolate, or perhaps soup ladled into tiny orange pumpkins to be cradled

RIGHT: *Let it rain or snow. When glass replaces screening, the vagaries of Mother Nature are no problem. Furniture, fabrics, and rugs appreciate the security of an enclosed porch.*

in the hands. For an easy, healthy snack, you can't go wrong with a big bag of popcorn and a metal popcorn popper that can ride over the flames. Listening to the bursts and pops is almost as much fun as actually devouring the finished product. Without carpeting to fret about, it doesn't matter if the buttered kernels travel or if the revelers track in leaves or wet snow, the first white flakes of a brand-new equinox. Just pull a hearth bench up close to the fire, and warm your toes.

## Porch Maintenance

Despite the wake of clothes and crumbs, porches abhor housecleaning. After all, the porch is where we come to relax, not to do housework. Happily, only minimal measures need to be taken; a quick neatening to restore a semblance of order, a light sweeping, and an occasional mopping (with an earth-friendly soap) are enough. Pillows should be regularly shaken or beaten to rid them of dust or pollen. And

rugs need the same, although the cotton ones can be thrown in the washer. When spiderwebs, looking like lace doilies, surface at rafter height, pull out your feather duster—the one with the seven-foot (2.1m) handle (also good for buffing the ceiling fan)—and whisk them away.

The general rule for painting porch furniture is once every other year, even less often with industrial paints, which contain more binders for adhering the paint to surfaces. In between these bouts, even the most fastidious recommend only that you enjoy. Nature likes to stir things up, and such elements as pine needles, dandelion fluff, and sand will all make appearances. It's an endless cycle, so give in.

ABOVE: *While screened porches seem to exist in a state of limbo between the interior of the home and the surrounding environment, there are various decorative measures that will emphasize the space's outdoor nature. Here, wicker furnishings and plants do the trick. Despite the outdoor ambience, the space stays up and running during inclement weather.*

CHAPTER THREE

# Basking in Privacy

O N A SULTRY AFTERNOON WHEN ALL THE WORLD SEEMS STILL, A porch—especially a more private one—becomes a much-appreciated retreat. Often situated at the back or the side of the house, the private porch is as essential to our well-being as the public porch where we entertain. Hidden from traffic and passersby, we sit enthralled by the sound of buzzing bees or the heady scent of the garden. This is most likely the place to which we'll come to share a secret with a friend, to steal a lover's kiss, or just to linger in a bathrobe and let our wet hair dry in the sun. If we've taken the day off, we don't have to advertise. Intimate and secret, these Zen-like outdoor spaces are special hideaways for rejuvenation and relaxation. With a tall lemonade, we can swing aimlessly on the glider or sway gently in a deep hammock and let the rest of the world—like the very ice in our glass—melt away.

A tucked-away escape requires little, but benefits from almost anything that makes you happy. Come the weekend, raise a paper kite in the yard, tie the string to a porch pillar, and spend all afternoon watching the bright triangle soar; bake a pie, and set it out to cool under its own prim little mesh dome; brew a pot of herbal tea, and sip it from an heirloom porcelain teacup, the cup you rarely take down from the shelf. A complete life, someone wise once said, means making time to enjoy the simple things. Think of a porch or a corner of a porch as a still life, and compose it as such. The goal is to create a setting where a perfect ripe peach can be shared, a flower contemplated, and a poem read aloud and savored.

ABOVE: *Located at the back of the house, this porch serves as a cozy hideaway. Serene retreats such as this allow us to commune with nature or a friend unobserved.*

OPPOSITE: *A classic folding lounge chair provides a comfortable spot for quiet musings. The sling-shaped form hugs the body, and the canvas material is easily brushed clean.*

## Creating Privacy

Privacy, a precious commodity not to be taken lightly, is attainable on any porch. While the location and surroundings of some porches may provide all the privacy you could ask for, other porches may not automatically afford you this luxury. But whether you want to feel protected from the gaze of nosy neighbors or create a cozy nook that feels secluded from the rest of your outdoor room, there are many ways to achieve the desired result.

## LIVING BORDERS

To cultivate a whimsical and charming setting that encourages peaceful repose, look to nature and put her wondrous gifts to work. A twig trellis or a lattice screen can be situated at one or both ends of a porch, or even somewhere in the middle, to provide the framework for a barrier of greenery and blossoms. Marry either of these easy-to-install fixtures with a hardy climbing rose, such as the pale pink 'New Dawn', or a zealous green vine and, suddenly, the porch, or a section of it, becomes an enchanting refuge, dappled with sunlight and perfumed with flowers.

Although we usually call upon such celebrated perennial climbers as fast-growing clematis, an ivy-covered trellis will also make a verdant shield. Even on a winter afternoon, with the sun hanging low in the sky, an ivy wall will afford pretty protection so that we can sit and dream of summer, unobserved. And enthusiastic ivy can be counted on to grow thicker and taller as the years pass. A flower-filled planter on casters or a potted tree (which can be underplanted with impatiens and begonias) can also be employed to subdivide a large porch or shield a small one from neighbors. These alternatives come with the added bonus of mobility, allowing you to change the setup of your porch at will.

If your porch faces a busy street, complete with all the noisy disturbances you're trying to avoid, don't give up hope. A row of generously planted window boxes will make the hullabaloo seem to disappear. Crammed full of portly geraniums, festive zinnias, marigolds, or begonias, the boxes form a bountiful barrier that's beautiful no matter which side you're on. A small planter of eager black-eyed Susan vine with its own attached trellis does away with the traffic and jazzes up the porch with its white, yellow, or orange flowers.

The boxes themselves can be painted to match the porch railings or done up in a complementary color. Although terra-cotta and wood are the most popular choices for these containers, metal,

BELOW: *Sumptuous vines shield a private sitting area and provide a lush green backdrop. Pretty on both sides, the dense greenery pleases the neighbors—and makes them disappear. White wicker furnishings, a low planter filled with annuals, and a fern set atop its own stand infuse the corner with romantic airs.*

fiberglass, and polymer endure far longer and come in all sorts of configurations and hues. Some containers are even designed to be self-watering, which leaves you with more time to sit and admire them.

Use metal brackets to affix the boxes to porch railings. Or, if the railings are wide and flat on top, line up a dozen or two flower pots in varying sizes instead (just make sure that they're heavy enough so that they won't blow over in strong winds). Marching up and down like sentinels, the pots (some painted, some plain) will provide a shield that's just as attractive and effective as boxes. The growing, blooming barricade harbors you in the most gracious way possible, all the while keeping the neighborhood's best interests in mind.

OPPOSITE: *Both of this home's porches are effectively screened without seeming unfriendly. A rich hedge of striking red blooms forms a natural barrier at ground level, while pristine louvers provide privacy up above.*

ABOVE: *Thanks to a strategically planted row of burgeoning rhododendron bushes, this treasured haven seems worlds away from the busy street that lies only steps beyond. Air and light circulate through the leafy branches, but vistas of cars and pedestrians are banished.*

Hanging plants act much the same way. Strung along an urban front porch, hanging baskets of trailing ivy (or ivy trained on wire to grow vertically), scarlet fuchsia, and ferns obscure views of buildings and cars without completely erasing vistas of the sky or handsome trees that might be planted along a residential street. With some tactful scheming, it's possible to frame the views you want to keep (perhaps a neighbor's willow, the weathervane on a barn, the pointy top of an evergreen) and lose the ones you don't (a neighbor's homely doghouse, an uninspired cement building down the block, an unsightly telephone pole).

Set out a wooden baker's rack, a multitiered antique wire plant stand, or a brand-new, folding, shiny aluminum stepladder. Stocked with flower-filled pots, each becomes a faux wall without seeming heavy and cumbersome, and without diminishing the porch's spaciousness. The ladder in particular is easy to fold up and move about from place to place, while a recycled stainless steel office trolley—loaded with green ferns—will seem to sail from one corner to the other. Like a magician, you want to establish the idea of a separate world, not obliterate the existing one. An extra box of heliotrope, an inch this way or that with your chair, and you've created a whole different scene.

BELOW: *Soaking up the sun, a pair of comfy, oversize wicker chairs present themselves poolside. Later in the day, perhaps to grab a nap or finish a novel, the owners can pull the long drapes shut for greater intimacy.*

## OTHER SCREENS

Setting up plant barriers is not the only way to achieve a sense of seclusion. Awning fabric sewn with rings and hung from simple hooks presents an instant fortress. And shades of all sorts—rattan, bamboo, wood, canvas—can easily be installed with metal hooks along the front or sides of a porch and raised or lowered when desired. A shade of weather-resistant material will also be an able-bodied protector, deflecting sun and rain.

Of course, privacy on the porch doesn't necessarily mean solitude. Perhaps you'd like to

fashion a cozy spot for a romantic dinner for two. To create a sense of intimacy on a large porch, incorporate a set of canvas curtains falling from ceiling to floor. Set the table with a few candles and it's as though you're dining in a Turkish tent. Better yet, employ a low table, surround it with pillows, and you've got a scene right out of *The Arabian Nights*. When you want to open up this nook to the rest of the porch, simply tie the curtains back with heavy tasseled cords.

Folding screens are also generous providers of privacy. Perhaps you want an away-from-it-all retreat where you can stretch out to finish the best-seller you started

ABOVE: *Floor-to-ceiling curtains flutter in the breeze while shading this oasis from prying eyes. Hung on rods, the curtains can be flung open to catch the sun or discreetly shut for romantic dining. Pillows lavishly strewn about serve as portable seats and enhance the exotic flavor of the setting.*

FOLDING SCREENS ARE AN AGE-OLD REMEDY FOR THOSE WHO seek a private moment. And with that lineage comes a whole lot of personality. In many old movies, for instance, folding screens made of floral fabric make an appearance; the heroine dashes behind one to undress and flings one nylon stocking coquettishly overboard. Needless to say, these screens carry with them an aura of mystery and romance, just the thing for a private porch. In general, any sort of transportable screen is an incredibly accommodating porch companion. If you can hinge it, you have a screen.

Picture a screen fashioned out of old windows, salvaged wood panels, or doors. Louvered exterior window shutters (or wood shutters with cutouts) are perfect. Outdoor fixtures themselves, they naturally complement an outdoor room. Old ones will already be painted; leave them the way they are, or remove the loose paint with a wire brush and repaint. New ones will require priming before painting. Join two shutters by placing one hinge (stainless steel, brass, or black iron) a quarter of the way down from the top of the shutters and another hinge a quarter of the way up from the bottom. Then attach a third shutter. If three are too heavy, hinge just two,

but make several pairs so that you can construct an effective wall. If more height is required, have the shutters affixed to simple wood bases.

When it comes to fabric-covered screens, there are a number of options. Consider how much light you want to pass through the barrier. Sheer cloth will diffuse the light, while something like burlap will be a great sun-blocker. If you go with a screen fashioned from artist's canvas, you can decorate it however you desire. Free-hand painting, stenciling, and rubber-stamping are just a few of the ways you can lend such a screen character. Generally, a screen will have three panels. You may opt for one that has the same patterned cloth, front and back, or one that is, in effect, reversible, with different patterns on the different sides. The latter will afford you the opportunity to change the backdrop of your private retreat whenever the mood strikes.

Freestanding iron frames—such as old-fashioned hospital screens—are also light and pretty for a porch. Commission one from a local blacksmith. Fabric can be attached to the metal frame with fabric ties or laced with rope strung through metal grommets.

months ago or where you can snuggle with a drowsy child late in the day and read a soothing story. A folding screen can help create such a secluded sanctuary by effectively separating one corner from the more public areas of the porch or by blocking the view of outsiders. And since folding screens do just what they say, you can stretch them out when needed and shrink them when you want to let other people in on your secret. Place a wood screen on casters, and you've got a movable divider that can be zoomed wherever you wish to create an instant room—a niche for yourself when you need to pen a personal note, paint your toenails, or simply snooze undisturbed.

## The Trappings

Private spaces warm up to comfortable furniture. Each and every piece should extend an invitation to lounge. We need upholstered or cushioned armchairs that we can sink into for whole afternoons. But furniture doesn't have to be old and squishy to serve up such homey comfort. To intensify the spirit of quiet nurturing, each piece need only be compliant, enveloping, unbuttoned. There should be nothing that reminds us of sitting at a desk, nothing hard and unyielding. Instead, let us be tempted by wooden or canvas swings brimming with pillows in watermelon and peach shades, cozy settees, and come-hither lounges set in pairs so young-at-heart romantics can hold hands when

BELOW: *Private escapes call out for yielding furniture. Here, oversize chairs and matching ottomans encourage reclining and bathe occupants in a feeling of luxury. Head back, feet up—this is the life. Emphasize comfort with overstuffed cushions that make you and your guests feel pampered.*

RIGHT: *It's not just children who adore porch swings. The steady creak is music to adult ears, too. Here, a charming wooden version that matches the porch railing has been outfitted with a floral seat cushion and pale green pillows that suit the natural surroundings.*

BELOW: *A cushioned bench sidles up to the porch railing, which provides an instant backrest with the help of some toss pillows. The owners can sit and read or lie back and take in the sunset, adjusting the pillows to suit their needs. Notice how the long seat cushion mimics the colors of the sky's show.*

OPPOSITE: *Suspended above the floor, a hammock elevates both body and spirit. Choose one with decorative fringe, and load it with pillows—you'll find it's seldom unoccupied. Here, a white version was selected to match the other furnishings.*

the mood is right. A wooden swing in particular has the power to evoke strong feelings of nostalgia. If you own a garden bench, remove the legs and attach some metal chains for a quick-order swinging settee.

The king of porch relaxation is the hammock. Similar to the way you can hold a conch to your ear and hear the ocean, you can lie down on a hammock and feel the gentle rocking of waves. Anchored to its own iron stand or suspended from the ceiling, a hammock can act as a bed or a sofa.

Like seating, tables bring their own personalities to bear. While some are just for show, many are primarily for service, especially on private porches where space tends to be at a premium. Capable of being mounted to a wall, fold-away tables are handy space-savers. Pull one out when you sit down to pen a letter, and flip it back when you're done. A little round table—having just enough room for a glass of lemonade and a small bowl of berries—placed next to a single armchair declares that this is a spot for private reflection. Makeshift tables, such as a stack of wicker picnic hampers or a hefty tree trunk sawed to the right height, add character and make a private sitting area more personal. It doesn't matter if there are nicks showing on the antique bench you've enlisted as a coffee table or if the paint is chipping. Every chink is a testament to past reveries. Assemble your cast of tables and chairs according to what pleases you most and let them hobnob as they will.

Lay down a soft rag rug, one that can easily be laundered, for bare feet to nuzzle. Or paint the floor. Kicky blue and white stripes to hide flaws, a geometric border for punch, or perhaps green and white checks? A private porch is allowed to be a little quirkier than one that faces the street. And narrow floorboards painted in a checkered design will visually expand a small space and make it sing.

Color, it's well documented, affects the psyche. Yellow is said to promote well-being and increase energy, blue calms and relaxes, orange cheers, and green refreshes. Since we've come to the porch to slow down, to be at long last motionless and mellow, it's important that we choose the proper palette. The professionals tell us that to achieve serenity we need atmospheric greens and grays, natural earth tones, or filmy pastels. That's not to say we can't gather bouquets of plucky citrus shades or let it rip with fire engine red cushions. Allow the color of the house and its location to help you formulate a theme. For instance, such sherbet hues as lemon, lime, and raspberry are sure to cool the hottest of porch settings. Perfect partners for palms and tiles, these tropical tones will bounce off vistas of blue water and white sand.

All that said, we must also follow our inclinations. If purple is a color we require to feel restful, then we should bring it on in subtle prints and basic, reassuring stripes. We are the cultivators of this private world. If we desire a cozy feel, we can paint the porch's high ceiling in a dark shade to make it seem lower and more protective. If we blunder, we can repaint, recover, regroup. On a lazy-time porch, nothing is written in stone. Why not a turquoise Adirondack chair or a glass table with an iron base in deep pink? How about a rattan end table with an overlay of tiles in black (a color that encourages independence) to introduce a note of elegance? If you're uncertain, try the color in little doses first. You can always add more.

PAGE 72: *A powerful use of color rocks this oasis. A vivid marigold hue and a medium blue team up on the wall, similar hues pop up in the pillows and table covering, and striking pink blooms tumble down to create a captivating show. In the midst of the roar and rumble, two pristine white wicker chairs act like exclamation points.*

PAGE 73: *This screened porch exudes a feeling of serenity, thanks to the beautiful shade of blue that bathes not only the wall, but the louvered doors and the rocking chair as well. Touches of yellow—introduced by fruit and flowers—provide zings of sunshine.*

## Sun-ripened Details

The private porch lets us enjoy intimate familial moments as well as solitary ones. Here, the stuff of our common experiences can find a home. The constant tide of flotsam and jetsam that accumulates on windowsills and on tables is part of the atmospheric style of a porch. Family and friends go out for a walk and come home bearing souvenirs they've discovered along the route—shells, sea glass, milkweed, and pinecones. Incorporate their finds into the decor of a no-frills refuge and you bring personality to the place. To keep the stash tidy, put out baskets, buckets, and boxes. Heavier woven rectangular baskets, mounted on casters, become instant storage bins that can be stowed under a sofa. Open shelves by the door could hold a collection of favorite round beach stones or sun-bleached starfish. Metal or straw baskets tacked to the wall will make a place for dried flowers and such sundries as sunglasses, tubes of sunscreen, and decks of cards.

On a porch at the shore, the celebrity is going to be the large, clear, glass apothecary jar brimming with sea glass in all its breathtaking watery hues to catch the afternoon light like a prism. Filling this giant glass summer after summer becomes a ritual, and during the other three seasons, the collection triggers memories of sun-washed days spent combing the beach for treasures.

Don't forget, private porches are also frivolous spaces where you can indulge your wit. Why not hang a carved wooden fish (discovered at a tag sale), an old-time sign that posts the House Rules (the owner, of course, is always right), or a lifetime's collection of black lab memorabilia? To stir up a little conversation, dress a life-size mannequin in style, give it its own seat, and wait for your friends' reactions. Surrounding yourself with the keepsakes you love best, the things that make you smile, is another foolproof method for inducing relaxation. Mount a banner representing your beloved alma mater, or hang a framed flag that once flew from the stern of your grandfather's boat. If you have a broad swath of wall, show off a vivid crafts collection; keep fine art that could be damaged indoors, of course.

BELOW: *An assortment of whimsical bird-houses rests where the collector can most enjoy them. The teeny structures enhance the outdoor ambience, as does a carved wooden bird perched up above. Earth tones pervade the space, allowing the natural greenery beyond to shine.*

OPPOSITE: *It's impossible to walk along the beach and return empty-handed. Line up shells, bits of driftwood, or pieces of sea glass on porch ledges and railings. Displayed in the open, the treasures can be admired easily. When the collection grows too big, find a basket or clear bottle and load it up.*

# PERFECT BREWS

SOME DRINKS NATURALLY LEND THEMSELVES TO LIFE ON THE porch. Lemonade and iced tea, for instance, have leisure written all over them. While packaged varieties will do, home-made drinks bring the pleasure to new heights. Special enough to warrant your best glasses and sprigs of freshly picked herbs, these sweet brews are perfect for lingering over with a friend.

Lemonade, prepared the same way our grandmothers made it, is everyone's favorite. And sun tea, which requires more time but no energy, is the premium refresher on a swel-tering afternoon. Start your outdoor steeping after breakfast and by lunchtime you'll have beautiful honey-colored tea.

### LOVELY LEMONADE AND LIMEADE

For each serving, combine the juice of one good-size lemon with one cup of water and 4 to 5 teaspoons of sugar. A long, slender-looking lemon will yield more juice than a fat, round one. Before squeezing, roll the fruit quickly back and forth between the palm of your hand and a flat surface. The motion loosens the flesh, and the fruit will be juicier. Strain the lemon, water, and sugar mixture. Pour into glasses filled with ice. Garnish with a small sprig of fresh mint. To make limeade, follow the same steps, substituting one lime for each lemon. Sugar cookies—the ones you roll out and cut with a cookie cutter or drop by the teaspoon and flatten with a glass dipped in granulated sugar—are the perfect accompaniments.

### SUN TEA

Fill a clear glass pitcher or a large glass jar with cold water. According to how strong you prefer your tea, suspend several tea bags (China or Earl Grey) over the side, making sure they are well immersed. Cap the jar or cover the pitcher, set it in full sun, and go meet some friends. In a couple of hours, the sun will have warmed the water enough to have steeped the tea. The result is an exceptionally clear, amber-colored drink. Remove the tea bags, add lemon, sugar, and fresh mint as you like to each glass, but keep the pitcher of sun tea pure so you can admire its hue all afternoon. If you're not a fan of mint, use a sprig of lemon balm instead. (Lemon balm, a cousin to laven-der, has a strong lemon scent but only when it's fresh, so don't bother to dry it.) Finger sandwiches of thin slices of cucumber, a wisp of butter, and freshly ground black pepper are equally elegant with cold tea as well as hot. Slice off the crusts, and cut the sandwiches diagonally to form neat triangles. For the perfect finishing touches, lay out an array of slender iced tea spoons and linen napkins near a centerpiece of blowsy roses.

ABOVE: *A gardenlike porch is an ideal setting for sipping a cool, refreshing beverage.*

While the aforementioned accessories provide visual and tactile delights, don't forget your other senses. After all, you're out on the porch not only to take in the sights, but to breathe in the fresh air, savor the sweet scents of nearby blossoms and the distinctive aroma of cut grass, and listen to the serenades of chirping birds. When it comes to soothing sounds, there is little that can top the sound of moving water. The gentle splashing of a fountain can be therapy for the soul. So wall-mount a small lion's head to spout a stream near the porch steps, or park a simple stone fountain there.

ABOVE: *Paying no heed to convention, this porch plays host to a couple of prized treasures not typically seen on a porch. An oversize lobster—appropriate for the waterfront location—and an intricately painted chest of drawers look as happy as clams paired with white wicker chairs and bright geraniums.*

Even a tabletop copper or ceramic fountain will produce hours of pleasing porch music. Equipped with their own pumps, these self-contained water environments can simply be plugged into a porch outlet. Lean back on the soft pillows, close your eyes, and really listen. The melody should be no more and no less than a whisper. If you are late for an appointment—just this once—the world will forgive you.

Wind chimes and wind gongs play a different tune. Some strike a resonant bong with each breeze, some are more tinkling and fairylike. But on a porch—especially one planned for introspection—a wind chime should be somewhat restrained. Too much clanging will jangle the nerves, so choose carefully. When the lights go out, a small, delicate wind chime can bring an extra dimension to the night's own symphony. If the noise becomes overpowering, move the chimes to a nearby tree. Different varieties can be made of metal, ceramic, or laboratory-grade borosilicate glass. Which one to choose? It's really a personal decision—similar to picking out wedding music. Most chimes and gongs include a magnet that can be used to silence the wind-catchers should the wind whip them up to a crescendo.

## *Double-duty Porches*

Occasionally, a more private porch also serves as a connector or entry. Whether adjoining the kitchen, surrounding the back door, or linking the main living areas of the house with the guest quarters, such a porch must be functional as well as nurturing. Boots and sporting gear, for example, are shed shamelessly on the porch near the back door. The small side porch opening to the kitchen is where the cook—escaping from the hot room—will sit to shell the peas or husk the corn for dinner, which will result in errant tassels and pods. And firewood for the living room inevitably ends up on the porch in a heap, shedding its dry bark like trees do leaves. To maintain the appealing atmosphere of harmony and seclusion, weave these domestic occurrences into the setting. Such daily rituals as putting out a bowl of water for the dog needn't detract from the scene. And sometimes, given a significant twist, the mundane trappings that accompany these simple occupations will enhance the coziness. In the words of nineteenth-century poet Charles Graham Halpine, "Don't despise the little things which happen daily round us, for some of them may chance take wings to startle and astound us."

Recruit a hardworking tin-topped table for the cook's chores, try stacking the firewood in a handsome basket, and install a peg rack for caps. Move in a rack for skis and one for mountain bikes. A stocky coatrack in the corner or a series of ceramic hooks will take care of slickers, while an umbrella stand will gladly swallow up a burgeoning

BELOW: *This diminutive back porch acts as a serviceable entry as well as a gratifying haven, thanks to the careful placement of a wicker table and matching chairs. Positioned off to the side of the doorway, safely out of the flow of traffic, the furnishings create a welcoming spot for sipping iced tea or reading the mail. A window box planted with red geraniums injects the tiny area with warmth.*

ABOVE: *Adjacent to the kitchen, a tiny back porch becomes a cook's private escape. And all it takes is a wicker chair and some strategically planted flowers. Spending a few minutes in this comfortable resting spot, gazing upon the pink flowers and savoring the gentle breeze, provides a soothing break from everyday chores.*

cluster of walking sticks, umbrellas, and tennis rackets. If this is where the cat likes his dinner served, let it be from a good-looking stoneware or stainless steel dish. Place the dish on a bright woven mat that matches the color of the porch pillows. Messy birdseed and pet food can be kept on the porch in galvanized cans or in decorative painted metal cans with tight-fitting lids. Bestow a metal scoop to each can in order to facilitate feeding. Or hang a whole collection of scoops in a row. Given the right position against a porch wall, even a simple wooden broom or a whole line of antique whisk brooms will become sculptural.

For final touches, add a thermometer (prominently displayed or not) so that every morning weather enthusiasts can check the temperature themselves without having to wait for the report on the radio. Find an out-of-the-way resting place for a dustpan to facilitate quick cleanups, and create a more noticeable spot for a giant blackboard with a tray full of chalk to record messages or to leave humorous notes for family members. And last but not least, put out an iron bell for visitors who wish to formally announce they're here to sit on the porch. Make it small—not school-bell size—so that it can serve as a gesture, not a command, and mount it on a porch post or on the wall of the house by the door. This is the bell you will ring, too, when you want the kids to come in for dinner or a spouse to come in from the garden. The sound of it clanging on the porch, drawing in the flock, will serve as a pleasant signal.

## Second Stories

Located high above street level, a second-story porch affords loads of privacy. Many older homes feature a good-size second-story porch, usually located directly above a first-floor porch or an enclosed sunroom at the corner of the home. From this comfortable perch, we are often greeted with surprising vistas that we never imagined at street level: a smudge of distant mountains, a green city park, a far-away hill covered in wildflowers, a wedge of azure ocean. Such views extend the boundaries of our world as we know it and speak of limitless possibilities.

Long before the advent of air-conditioning, in the days when women wore layers of petticoats and pinched their waists and men wore stiff collars, a sleeping porch was the antidote for hot summer nights. Seldom used for that purpose these days, except in the hottest climates, such elevated and screened spaces have become popular, lofty sitting rooms instead. Still beneficial in that they will naturally ventilate a bedroom or a whole second floor, letting night breezes swoosh in to cool the farthest corners, these screened porches are, by their very nature, dreamlike. On a warm night, lounging on one of these porches and listening to the rustle of the leaves, we're as happy as children marooned in a tree house.

Architecturally, sleeping porches will always evoke our emotions. Being held aloft, we feel uplifted. To foster the storybook feeling, these multipurpose aeries need only the

BELOW: *A savvy structural plan allows the roof of one porch to serve as the floor for another. While it mimics the style of the entry porch, the second-story retreat has something to offer that its counterpart does not—privacy. Suspended above street level, the cozy haven allows occupants to see everything without feeling as though they themselves are on display. A carefully chosen palette enhances the architecture and unites the porches.*

simplest decoration: comfortable chairs, soft fabrics, mounds of pillows. If company warrants using the porch as an occasional guest room, snowy linens that glow in the moonlight will be enough. For a makeshift yet beautiful canopy, suspend yards of diaphanous muslin over the bed. What could be more romantic than drifting off to sleep in the midst of such a dreamy setting, your last waking glimpses being of the starry sky above? A hammock is another worthwhile recruit. Launch a generously wide one where it will catch the earliest morning light, and lavish it with quilts or a Navajo blanket and pillows. Such thoughtful touches as a miniature night-light or a tray with a pitcher of ice water are always noted. These gestures augment our perception of being nurtured and comforted.

More like roofed balconies, the tinier second-story porches, those rarely able to hold more than two small chairs and a table, are—or should be—great time-out spaces for busy parents who covet a few valuable minutes alone. Whether perched high above a city street or suspended over a suburban garden, these minute structures are capable of enhancing the living quality and functionality of a bedroom. When the children are tucked in, couples can step outside and enjoy the night air without leaving home. Such a cozy spot is also a great place for sipping coffee and reading the paper early in the morning. A pair of hickory twig armchairs and a pot or two of white petunias or ivy—wall-mounted so as not to usurp space—will help elevate the fanciful feeling. A small gilded mirror will catch a bit of sky and visually expand the porch's perimeters.

OPPOSITE: *A wicker bed and pretty sheets imbue this cottage sleeping porch with a sense of tranquillity, while a blue and white color scheme and a model sailboat pay homage to the nearby sea. French doors keep the snug space feeling open and airy during the day, but at night, rod-hung curtains step in to provide privacy.*

BELOW: *Two chairs cozy up to each other on a small second-story porch designed as a couple's special hideaway. The lace-framed doorway and gauzy white pillow set a romantic mood.*

RIGHT: *The owners of this home have numerous places where they can relax and enjoy the fresh air. An expansive front porch has two separate sitting areas, while a second-story hideaway offers views far and wide. A half-moon opening frames the latter and serves as a soft counterpoint to the straight lines of the architecture below.*

BELOW: *An open railing maximizes the view and welcomes breezes onto the upper-level porch. Boxes of trailing plants enhance the vista, providing dashes of color.*

OPPOSITE: *The upper and lower porches not only provide different degrees of privacy, but exhibit slightly different personalities as well. Downstairs, a simple wooden rocker looks right at home with the straightforward columns. Upstairs off the bedroom, the mood is softer with wicker seats.*

Other than a wee carpet and a candle, there's not much room for anything else in this especially intimate type of outdoor space. But then the two of you—alone, no kids allowed—should prove enough. If the porch is screened, you can leave the door wide open all night to take advantage of the cooling wind. And if you wake up during the night, you'll see the flowers with their luminous petals fluttering like banners in the moonlight.

## The Spa Porch

The thrill of bathing outdoors in the early morning to the tune of melodious birds is a rapturous experience. We can hear the same trilling indoors through the open windows, but with the sopranos warming up right at our elbow, the score seems twice as lively. Soaking in the silver light of the moon is even more intoxicating. The addition of a hot tub transforms a porch into a sybaritic space. Immersed in the warm water with the stars in sight, we don't worry about what needs to be done tomorrow, the daily demands placed upon us, or the pressure of deadlines. Water, air, and time make up a no-fail recipe for healing a harried mind and a tired body. Seduced by the velvety texture of the water and the dark sky, we close our eyes and feel as though we're floating. This could be the quintessential moment of utter and complete relaxation—the porch as spiritual healer.

A wraparound porch is particularly suited for this sort of sensual activity. On such a porch, the tub can be tucked around a corner out of sight, making the bathing experience more private. But hot tubs can be discreetly blocked from view with fixed or movable screens as well. Masses of green tropical plants, a couple of healthy citrus trees in blue and white Chinese pots or wood planters, and canvas curtains will all render a hot tub more hidden, more exclusive, more enchanting. A few well-chosen flowers, a delicate rice-paper screen, and we have fashioned a hedonistic spa that gracefully fades from sight.

No less tantalizing, however, is a bath that is technically indoors, yet linked to a small covered porch of its very own. Contemporary architects often use this idea in planning master suites. A bath that includes access to a private porch or deck provides an excuse to linger longer, to revel. In warmer climates, such sensuous retreats are often planned in conjunction with a garden, each heightening the other's charm. A bather can view the porch and the flowers beyond—through a set of open French doors, for instance—and still have all the amenities right there at his or her fingertips. Indeed, it is worthwhile to plan what plantings will surround the tub. Some flowers such as exotic orchids seem to relish the steamy clime of the bath. Several pots of these beauties on the edge of the tub can make a lush and appropriate segue to such heady nocturnal outdoor bloomers as nicotiana, angel's trumpets, and stock. Each and every one floods the scene with fragrance. Cleopatra knew what she was doing when she had her chambers scattered with rose petals to the depth of a

wine glass. Seemingly without distinction and with so much perfume in the air, the porch, the garden, and the bath become one.

For such indoor-outdoor bathing and mind-cleansing, nothing says luxury like handfuls of thick cotton bath towels. Fold as many as you can into a handsome rattan basket, or stack a dozen neatly in an armoire. Opulence is key. White or cream-colored towels speak to the calm nature of this restorative process. There is no tolerance for jarring colors or unfriendly synthetic surfaces. Everything in these private havens should promote a sense of serenity. You want to move in slow motion and soak up the aura like a sponge. Wrap yourself in a soft robe, slip out on the porch, and inhale the night. A chaise—drifting halfway between the flower beds and the tub—makes a proper raft for counting stars or glow-in-the-dark petals.

Pragmatism has no place on this leave of absence. So forgo the usual ho-hum towel rack for an antique wooden ladder. Lean the ladder against the wall of the porch or the bath and use the rungs as towel bars. Recruit more candles for this spot, soft rugs, music, a small cabinet to hold the essentials: a corkscrew and wine glasses. After all, the Egyptian queen would most certainly agree, what better occasion on which to offer a toast or two?

OPPOSITE: *Beckoning from the back corner of a wraparound porch, this hot tub promises the ultimate in pampering. A row of plantings shields occupants from view while still allowing them to enjoy the breathtaking mountain scenery. The highly gracious porch also offers a place to dine with friends.*

ABOVE: *A hot tub sunken into its own little enclosed porch allows the owners to savor the beach environment as they soak in the soothing water. While the landscape provides a natural screen, curtains can be drawn for complete privacy. Soft towels, scented candles, and pillows for resting the head lend the experience a sense of luxury.*

## CHAPTER FOUR

# Dining Alfresco

ABOVE: *This breezy porch invites both gathering and dining. After meals, friends and family can either linger at the table or drift over to the wicker rockers and settee.*

OPPOSITE: *Protected from the hot sun as well as the rain, diners look forward to meeting under this lofty roof. A natural-fiber rug and earthy wicker chairs blend harmoniously with the architecture, while scores of green plants enrich the daily pageant.*

MAGINE SIPPING COFFEE, CRADLING THE WARM CUP IN YOUR HANDS AS the morning dew glistens on the grass, or picture sitting down to a candlelit supper of cold lobster with a full moon lighting a path on the water. Whether simple or elaborate, meals taken outside on the porch are feasts for all the senses. Barefoot or in formal dress, we are conscious of the magic. The food always tastes better, and the dining experience itself feels refreshing, as we are removed from the area in which we usually sit down to lunch or dinner. It is a combination of this change in routine, the fresh air, and captivating vistas that stimulates our appetites and invigorates our spirits. Transplanted to this outdoor environment, we perceive everything in a new light.

In those lucky regions where warm weather prevails year-round, this delightful method of dining can be a way of life. In less temperate areas, though, we have to make due with only a few fleeting months. Too impatient to wait for mild temperatures, we may venture out with the arrival of the first golden daffodils to munch our sandwiches; hunched in coats and armed with a thermos of coffee, we are nonetheless thrilled to break free of our winter confines and become reacquainted with this outdoor treat. Having been cooped up indoors too long, we approach the outdoor table with the same eager anticipation as when we go to take that first bite of a delectable dessert at the end of a meal.

Of course, having a picnic on the grass or the sand is highly enjoyable, but without a roof overhead or a floor below, we are vulnerable to such spirit-dampers as marauding ants and rain. On the porch, shelter and comfort are requisite side dishes.

Within steps of the kitchen, yet in spirit worlds away, a porch repast is a true banquet, one that combines the goodness of the food before us with the outdoor relaxation we so crave.

Picture a group of friends drawn around a porch table on a balmy summer evening. Perhaps they're sitting down to a scrumptious entrée of shiitake mushrooms with veal, an elegant dinner of saffron rice and shiny blue-black mussels, or such comforting fare as hot dogs and potato salad. The gastronomy can be as elaborate or as simple as we like. It's not really what we eat but the fact that we're eating out

BELOW: *A modernist sensibility dictates a streamlined table and chairs. Thanks to the pared-down furnishings, the sparkling pool takes center stage. Just make sure to wait half an hour after eating before jumping in.*

on the porch that matters. Drinking in the heady aromas, the incredible colors, we can let ourselves be engulfed by the day or the evening. When dinner is over and the coffee finished, conversation and candlelight will continue to hold us. Best of all, we know that each morning the cycle—breakfast, lunch, dinner—begins all over again. Breaking bread on the porch casts a powerful spell, drawing us back for meal after meal as long as the season lasts.

From a simple supper for two on trays to a catered luncheon for twenty, a vast array of occasions and social engagements can be accommodated on the porch. We can be lavish in our efforts or completely laid-back. Unlike an interior dining room, which often cannot comfortably play host to the number of people we've invited, a porch, whose boundaries are more forgiving, adapts. If the crowd grows too large, the party can simply spill onto the lawn or into the garden. When the extra guest shows up at the last moment, there's always a railing to sit on or steps to plop down on. Squeeze in that second card table, or mark a new place with a big, soft pillow. A good time can be had simply sitting cross-legged on a blanket spread out on the floor, picnicking on sandwiches while the crickets chirp and the kids run happily in and out of the sprinklers. Such casual yet fun-filled get-togethers often leave us with lasting impressions that are as powerful as those made by affairs we spent months planning. Ultimately, outdoor dining rooms are all about entertaining both guests and ourselves in the most comfortable ways possible. We should feel gladdened and relaxed, satisfied but not sated—similar to the effect of a perfectly balanced menu.

What to cook for hungry family and friends? This matter can be left to the chef's discretion. Seasonal offerings—fresh and prepared with a minimum of bother—are in keeping with an open-air meal, whether it be a Sunday brunch or a weekday dinner. Hit the market early, and improvise. Think of summertime food and the culinary offerings of Italy, southern France, and other Mediterranean areas. Think quick-fix—fruits, salads, and soups. Outdoor meals are perfect candidates for garnishes of flowers and fresh herbs. Involved sauces, complicated casseroles, and risk-taking combinations, on the other hand, are better saved for indoor cold-weather meals. Wait until the garden sleeps and the beach closes down before doing anything that will keep you in the kitchen for longer than an hour. Moments of leisure on the porch are far too dear to be squandered on a stew, even the most savory kind.

BELOW: *An outdoor room can be as lavish as an indoor one. This open-air living-dining room is chock full of furnishings. There's even a massive cupboard for storing dinnerware and displaying favorite objects. Windsor chairs, tall candlesticks, and a floral tablecloth lend the dining area elegance. Notice how the table covering echoes the fabric on the sofa, tying the two areas together.*

## *Setting the Stage*

When the doors to the porch open, the house expands with an almost audible sigh of relief. Suddenly, you acquire extra room for all sorts of activities, but maybe none so pleasurable as dining. And there are as many types of dining areas—and ways to dine—on a porch as there are dishes and cuisines to serve. With some clever planning, you can achieve a sense of festivity, seclusion, or romance. Traditional porch elements such as over-hanging roofs, lattice screens, and flower-laden trellises help form backdrops that can be either casual or formal. Such pockets of tranquillity transport you and your guests away from the hustle and bustle of everyday life. Why even consider setting an indoor table when the table on the porch overlooks a garden? But like campers moving out to stake claim to new ground, before you lay out any furniture, you should consider the direction of the sun, whether the wind picks up in the afternoon, and what path the rain usually takes. If the porch is your haven for only a few prized months, you'll want to maximize the extent of its use during that precious window. Undoubtedly, there will be adjustments and rearrangements, but familiarizing yourself with the basics will make for better results and, in the end, afford you extra time for savoring meals on the porch.

OPPOSITE: *A vine-covered pergola shades diners below. The earth-toned teak furniture and terra-cotta tile floor heighten the natural feeling of the outdoor space, as do slender potted trees. As is the case in a well-spiced dish, each element plays tastefully against the next.*

ABOVE: *The afternoon light spills across a stately columned porch. Family and guests can take their meals at the round table in the foreground or move back against the wall to dine in dappled shade. In the sitting area, plates are balanced on laps, while drinks rest on the coffee table. The substantial amount of space between the two areas gives each a sense of definition.*

### FINDING THE SPOT

Certain types of porches offer a number of potential locations for a dining area. If you have an L-shape porch, you may want to outfit one side as a living room and the other as a dining area. Or, perhaps you'd rather set up a gathering area at one end of the front expanse, create an eating area at the other, and reserve the side for private relax-ation. If you have a wraparound porch, you have numerous possibilities from which to choose. Again, take into account the time of day you'll be using your outdoor din-ing spot, the kind of light the prospective area receives during that time, and the view.

On a large veranda, one big dining table in the middle of the porch not only serves as a stunning gathering point, but also makes the large space feel more intimate. Chairs, matched or not, can come and go like weekend guests. Should you prefer to reserve the center portion of your porch for other activities, set up a dining area in one corner with a table and a built-in bench or two. Sharing a seat, diners feel instantly connected. If the seats have lids that lift up, they become handy hideaways for table linens, cushions, or candles. Built-ins are space-savers, which makes them especially helpful on smaller porches where order and versatility matter even more.

A rambling porch can benefit from a series of small dining areas, especially when the number of people dining often exceeds eight. This type of setup also helps to foster a sense of intimacy in a large space. Place the tables out of the flow of the busiest zone but close to one another so that no group feels isolated. Try to give each a glimpse of the flower beds or the green lawn. The important thing is to make the arrangements of tables and chairs equally comfortable and inviting—don't slight one grouping to benefit another. To tie the dining areas together visually, lay matching rugs underneath each table, cover the chair cushions in matching fabric, or paint the furnishings

BELOW: *This spacious poolside porch incorporates both a dining area and a living area. The side-by-side companions live in harmony with each other thanks to their common use of white wicker pieces. However, although there is no physical barrier between the two, a sense of separation is established by the orientation of the furnishings.*

of all the groups in a similar color. This type of setup is great for entertaining guests. Should you sense that one table may be more congenial than another, do as expert hostesses advise: when dessert and coffee roll around, ask that your guests swap seats. Such an unexpected and enjoyable relocation (almost always easier to accomplish outside than inside) sparks conversation and helps guests get to know one another better.

To create a dining area on a small porch, consider using a lightweight table that can be placed against a wall or railing when not in use, thereby opening up space for other porch pleasures. When it's time for a meal, the table can then be pulled out to accommodate seating on all sides. For this type of arrangement, you may want to use scaled-down stools that will slide underneath the table when not needed. Folding chairs, which can collapse and disappear into a corner until dinner time, are another space-efficient option. For a young couple longing to eat their after-work meal outdoors, a folding table nestled against a shingled wall and two folding bistro chairs may be all that is necessary. Folding chairs with wooden slats riveted to metal frames look particularly partylike when outfitted with two small cushions—one that fits against the backrest and one on the seat.

ABOVE: *A savvy placement of rugs or floorcloths can define a porch's activity areas. Place one vivid cloth or rug underneath the dining table and another in front of the sofa. The colorful additions—like flowers in a border—needn't match.*

## AN AIR OF DISTINCTION

If your porch serves a number of functions, you may want to give the dining area a sense of definition. To section off a dining spot from the rest of the space, you can call upon many of the same tricks used for fashioning private escapes. Folding screens and lattice dividers both make excellent partitions. The latter can be covered with winding vines or left bare and then painted a favorite color. While white lattice is almost unbeatable for a cool, summery dining retreat, a snappy color can brighten up an otherwise dark corner. And in warm climates, tropical hues can look right at home.

On a porch that houses both a dining spot and a living area, you may want to go with a great room effect and leave them open to each other. This type of arrangement promotes a feeling of togetherness. People at the dining table eating their breakfast, for instance, can still engage in idle chitchat with others reclining on a chaise or sitting on the porch swing. Remember, the porch is a place of leisure, and there are no rigid schedules. Late-morning risers can dive into a hearty breakfast while still enjoying the company of those who have moved on to other porch pastimes.

The lack of a physical partition, however, does not mean that you can't give each area its own air of distinction. Just like in an indoor great room, there are a number of techniques you can employ to give each space a sense of individuality. Color, the orientation of the furnishings, and the careful placement of area rugs can all be used to establish a subtle sense of distinctiveness. If you decide to go with different colors for each area, make sure that those colors are compatible.

## SHELTER

Certain measures can be taken to make your meals on the porch more enjoyable. Along the shore, where evenings sometimes brew up winds of squall-like ferocity, a partially enclosed area will make all the difference. Two walls of glazing meeting at the corner of a large porch will form a protected dining area snug enough to withstand the occasional unfavorable elements. The candles set on a table in this cloistered nook will continue to burn, unruffled by the same bracing wind that flattens the dune grass and tops the waves with whitecaps. On a calm night, if the glass windows are on tracks, they can be slid apart to usher in the sound of the sea and the soft, well-behaved breezes.

But the coast is not the only place where such a setup can come in handy. In areas that experience a change of seasons, a permanent elbow of glass will allow dining early in the spring and late into autumn. Sheltered from cold gusts, which are almost always what send us scurrying inside with our dinners half-eaten, we can enjoy leisurely meals on the porch well before and after the warm season. Another bonus: such a setting gives us the opportunity to spend plenty of time just sitting and monitoring the changes that each month brings to the landscape. A dark gray sea in early spring when the first fishermen begin to line the shore will give way to a vivid blue ocean come midsummer; mountains will lose their summer persona to the brilliant autumnal reds and oranges just when we're filling the bowls with shiny apples. At breakfast, the sky fades from russet to azure;

BELOW: *A clear glass barrier protects the porch from the wind and saltwater spray without diminishing the view. Although the glazing here is used to shield a lounging area, a similar setup could be applied to an outdoor dining room.*

over dinner, the first star makes its appearance. Witnessing these subtle alterations brings us closer to the world around us.

Of course, shades of all kinds can also define a space for dining and offer protection from the blazing sun or the wind. One of the worst scenarios you could have on the porch is a table full of people who are being blinded by the glare of the setting sun. Sunsets, sunrises, and even rain showers (which often entail a dreamy rainbow or produce theatrical effects in the sky) should be part of the daily entertainment—joys to behold, not trials to be endured.

Keep in mind that drapes or shades visible from a porch-facing interior room should complement that indoor room. (Likewise, interior shades that can be seen from the porch should work with, not against, your outdoor decor). Easily hung from rollers or simple hooks, shades can go up and down, or across, at a moment's notice

and can take up residence just about anywhere we want them to. If the porch openings are large, use two or more shades in a space. Doing so will give you the flexibility of having one shade open and one closed, thereby granting you greater control over how much light the porch receives. Curtain rings situated at both the top and bottom of an awning and gathered onto rods (similar to the arrangement of a curtain hung on a door) will keep the fabric from flapping about wildly. Retractable acrylic panels are weather-resistant, and awnings halt the midday glare. And such accessories as hanging baskets, flower-filled planters, a potted tree, or a mobile grid of shelves will filter sunlight with equal aplomb while providing privacy as well. By manipulating the light, you can heighten the drama of dining outdoors. Plus, leafy and bloom-filled protectors will bring you even closer to nature as you linger over your scrambled eggs.

## Tables and Chairs

As is the case with other porch furnishings, the pieces you single out for dining should be capable of living in harmony with the milieu and standing up to the elements. They should also reflect your taste and style. And, perhaps most importantly, furnishings should be comfortable. If you and your guests are to be whisked away from everyday cares, you can't be yearning for a soft backrest or a curved seat.

Materials range from cast iron and aluminum to various types of wood, such as teak, cedar, and redwood. While cast-iron pieces tend to be painted with a protective coat that will undoubtedly demand touch-ups, aluminum furnishings require less maintenance. In keeping with our demand for comfort and style, many manufacturers are offering chairs that are as ergonomically correct as they are inviting. A well-stocked shop that specializes in such pieces will have the whole range: teak to metal with weather-resistant cushions and pads to match.

Salvaged objects can take on new life on the porch and inject the area with a refreshing bit of unpredictability. A handsome old refinished door or an expanse of glass set atop a pair of slender iron sawhorses makes a beautiful dining spot. Or what about a recycled garden gate, painted white, mounted on a base, and topped off with glass for a light and airy feeling?

BELOW: *A cozy love seat and a pair of overstuffed chairs pull up to a table to make dining a regal experience. A purple and gold palette enhances the luxurious ambience. Notice how the color scheme pervades the space, appearing in the balloon shades, the tablecloths, the upholstery, and even the glass bowls and goblets. Setting up a dining area on an enclosed porch such as this allows you to enjoy "alfresco" meals regardless of the weather or time of year.*

Picnic tables also present an informal and inexpensive alternative. The wood can be painted white or left to weather to a driftwood tone. With seat cushions tied to the top of each long bench, the picnic table moves up a notch from its lowly backyard position. Benches of all sorts are ideal dining companions because they're easily stored under the table after a meal.

Round tables, which promote conversation, can make a small space appear larger, as can glass-topped tables. Diners feel less constricted if they don't have to maneuver around sharp corners. While rough, unmilled sticks—bark optional—would make a

ABOVE: *A step above its backyard counterparts, this picnic table and its matching benches display a refined rusticity. Echoing the construction of the log home, the pieces are completely worthy of their surroundings. Thanks to this harmony between furnishings and architecture, the setting has an air of tranquillity— ideal for indulging in leisurely meals.*

fitting base for an Arts and Crafts–inspired circular table with a down-home flavor, a round tabletop placed mushroomlike on a pedestal base (not legs) is far more comfortable and will help to foster a sense of airiness in a small setting. Imagine a round table artfully situated in a sun-dappled corner of a pristine porch. Come night, drape it with a floor-length cloth, lay out the silver, and it's a polished retreat. Not just a place to get off your feet, such a dining haven is a fine reason for uncorking the champagne and dishing out the caviar. Maybe beneath the cloth sits a mediocre table in need of paint, but who will notice? Add some flowers and candlelight, and the mood is complete.

And don't underestimate the charm of dining at the coffee table. If you're pressed for space, a generously sized coffee table can be the focal point for four chairs, serving as both an enticing gathering spot for shooting the breeze and a pleasant area for casual dining. Guests can park their glasses on the coffee table and hold their plates in their laps. Or big cushions can be laid on the floor as seats, and dining can take on a somewhat exotic flair. Such informal approaches are what make outdoor dining so appealing. Be sure the table has a finish that will stand up to water and spills. If there's room, set the salad and a loaf of crusty bread on the coffee table for easy access; fresh fruit for dessert and an assortment of cheeses can be arranged on a little side table. With all the necessities close at hand, no one will yearn to be sitting at a traditional dining table.

Unlike a coffee table, most tables at which we take meals require chairs or benches. While tables and chairs can be purchased as sets, one does not need to strictly match the other. Maybe it's just the materials that are similar, or style or colors. Outdoor chairs that lend themselves to alfresco dining come in a bountiful assortment of styles and shapes. The wrought-iron variety alone can be as streamlined as a sports car or as frilly as a doily. But if you're planning on using garden chairs—or those kitschy metal kitchen chairs you bought at a tag sale—measure to be certain their seats are at the right height for comfortable seating at your table.

ABOVE: *A circular table nestles snugly into the rounded end of a porch. To further foster a sense of intimacy, as well as to make the most of the available space, curved benches take the place of chairs. Notice how their slatted backs mimic the porch railing to create a seamless look—an effect that is enhanced by the use of white paint.*

OPPOSITE: *Coffee tables make fine dinner partners. Highly versatile, they can act as serving stations one day and as dining surfaces the next. At the moment, this one serves as a resting spot for plates, napkins, and glasses. The elegant tray and silver basket match the refinement of the table for a unified look.*

As is the case with seating in the living areas of a porch, slipcovers are a great unifying element. For a party, when all kinds of chairs are called into commission, easy-to-wash slipcovers (especially when they're sewn to fit loosely) can quickly be popped over all chair types—director's chairs, bentwood chairs, metal chairs—to iron out the differences. Slipcovers can also be used to imbue plain or informal chairs with a touch of elegance. Last but not least, these devices can be called into action when you simply want a little change of scenery. Put some on for a fancy anniversary dinner, then take them off in the morning when the kids show up. In general, roomy slipcovers work better with sunny beach cottages, while fitted ones go well with modern surroundings. Keep in mind, though, that a slipcover doesn't ensure comfort. For that element, you might need to pad the seat with a cushion. And make sure the design of the chair is conducive to relaxing. Try out a new chair the same way you would a mattress—by giving it a test run; sit in it, lean back, and put up your feet. Lots of times, outdoor diners show up in shorts or bathing suits, so it's important that the surface and material of the chair be as comfortable as the construction. Often, just an extra cushion or two can make a big difference.

## Style

What will the tone of your dining area be? For instance, do you want it to be casual or dressy? When making this decision, think about the kinds of occasions for which you'll be using the space. Will you be taking advantage of the spot primarily for quiet family-only meals, or do you plan on entertaining there often and hosting numerous outdoor parties?

When it comes to settling upon the look of the dining area, you can also take your cues from the natural setting or from the architecture of the house. Certain furnishings and architectural styles just seem to go hand in hand. Who can't envision wicker on the porch of a Victorian, ladder-back chairs on a Colonial, or slatted mahogany chairs on the porch of a slick contemporary dwelling? But contrasts don't negate beauty, and there's no rule that you have to be conventional. Experimentation is often the key to success. Some porches—old or new—might call for an uncluttered look. If you prefer this style, a guileless table and chairs—no extra pillows, no take-notice colors—are the way to go. Instead of color or fabric, concentrate on line and proportion. Think of angles, and import a piece or two that will offset the predominant horizontal lines

of the floorboards and vertical lines of the railing. In a situation such as this, the graceful curves of a chaise longue will do quite nicely. Remember, the ancient Romans took their meals reclining. If you want your morning coffee and muffin in a chaise, by all means incorporate one—or several to share this indulgence with others. Dual chaises with a table in between will make a fine way station for cocktails.

Outdoor dining rooms embrace the unexpected, which is another reason we love them. Paint a medley of iron chairs in bright primary colors for a bungalow, order a set of polka-dot seat cushions for a quartet of high-minded teak armchairs, recruit a vintage 1930s enamel-porcelain drop-leaf table with a quirky stencil design for breakfast by the back door. Out on the porch, we tend to try things we would never dream

ABOVE: *While this enclosed porch features plenty of living room furnishings—from cushioned rocking chairs to wing chairs to a sofa—the dining table boasts a position of prominence, situated at the center of the space. Wooden chairs decked out in a festive floral-patterned fabric give meals a celebratory feel. Overhead, a ceiling fan keeps diners cool.*

of doing inside the house. How about lacquering an old table in lilac or hand-painting butterflies on the backs of chairs? Maybe it's the fresh air that motivates us to trust our instincts. Less stilted on the porch than we would be planted indoors, we open like the very flowers around us. And if one day the porch seems too full, too overflowing with trinkets, do as the French designer Coco Chanel advised: simply remove one thing and you'll feel instantly better.

Basically, the bones of your outdoor dining area can be cloaked in any style as long as the space is welcoming. The true goal? Family and friends so relaxed and at ease that they settle in at the table content to wait all night for the shrimp bisque to cool or the rolls to arrive. This could be accomplished with just a lot of fat cushions to lean back on and a pretty view. If yours is an urban setting without mountains or water to study, shape a custom view: move in pots of flowering plants, a pretty screen, and an oversize mirror to reflect the clouds and surrounding greenery. Some foliage, some scent, and we are momentarily released into a different world.

*ABOVE: Mimicking the style of the table and chairs, a large hutch steps in to perform multiple tasks. The piece offers open shelving for books and display objects, drawers for flatware, and cabinets for linens and platters. At party time, this versatile furnishing functions as a buffet, allowing guests to help themselves and then gravitate to the tables.*

*OPPOSITE: A buffet setup keeps meals easy, whether you're hosting a party of fifty or a cozy lunch for four. Here, a long table dressed in sunny blue and yellow offers an array of salads as well as the necessary tableware. A short distance away, a round table with a spectacular view awaits the lunchers.*

## Entertaining Made Easy

Even when we're entertaining guests, we want to feel as relaxed as possible. And there's no reason that entertaining should be any more stressful than other porch activities. There are a number of things you can do to make entertaining on the porch easier while still ensuring that a good time is had by all.

### BUFFETS

Porches and buffets go together naturally, and allow us to assemble greater numbers for a meal. Plus, buffets remove the problem of the host having to constantly get up and down to serve guests. Instead, guests simply help themselves. And they will appreciate the opportunity to take only the foods that they want, and as much or as little as they prefer.

If you have room, incorporate a sideboard or hutch onto the porch for these occasions. Both have the added bonus of providing storage space for all sorts of porch odds and ends. A smaller, more narrow table placed up against the exterior of the house will also work. And don't forget benches and wide ledges on porch railings, both of which make great serving stations. If you simply have no space, don't be discouraged. Set up the food in the kitchen along with a stack of trays off to the side. Portable and playful, reminiscent of school days, trays can be left plain or topped off with colorful linens. These handy devices also provide a terrific solution to the problem of not having a table that is large enough to accommodate all your invitees. Once they've prepared their trays, guests are very adept at finding their own favorite places to sit—perhaps a wicker settee, the porch steps, a bench in the corner with a prime view of the horses grazing in the pasture. You could also scatter a few folding chairs and some fifties-style tray tables across the porch to create some additional perches.

For a successful buffet, serve a few main dishes and a salad at the same time rather than having a bunch of separate courses so that people aren't constantly getting up. Or coordinate a community porch supper, when the honeysuckle on the trellis is at

BELOW: *Keeping up with a long table that draws crowds for special meals, a lengthy tiled counter hugs the far wall. Designed for entertaining, the feature includes both open and concealed storage as well as a sink, enabling the host to use the area not only for serving, but also for meal preparation and clean-up tasks. The long-wearing tile is impervious to spills and welcomes activity. Off to the side, a hutch provides additional storage space and an extra serving spot.*

its peak, and instruct your guests on what to bring. By handing out individual assignments, you'll avoid duplicate offerings as well as gaps—no host or hostess wants to end up with three salads and no drinks. Dessert (your task) can also be staged buffet style. Fresh fruit is always welcome but offering something a little more decadent as well—for instance, sliced peaches and key lime pie (one from your favorite bakery is fine) or raspberries in heavy cream and chocolate cake—gives guests the best of both worlds.

## SPECIAL FEATURES

Special accoutrements such as built-in bars, with or without sinks, and built-in grills elevate the easy-living aura of a porch and facilitate entertaining for large groups. Hidden behind shutterlike double doors, a bar could include glass shelves for bottles and glasses as well as a sturdy pull-out or pull-down panel that functions as a surface for mixing drinks. Below, a small refrigerator or a built-in ice chest equipped with a drain

could hold beverages for an invite-the-whole-neighborhood cocktail party. Porch cocktail parties are always successful because they naturally time themselves to the light. Descending darkness subtly reminds those guests who may be inclined to stay on that it's time to depart.

Built-in grills and rotisseries that require special venting are most often found on contemporary porches. Immune to the weather and within close proximity of a kitchen, these are heaven-sent additions for grilling enthusiasts who love to cook but don't want to leave the party to tend the barbecue. Often featuring built-in shelves or even drawers, these hardworking stations can provide storage space for such necessities as cooking utensils, corkscrews, aprons, and mitts. Make a list of the items you always reach for, and find a place to stash them so that you're well equipped at all times.

On a far less grand scale, bottles of soda and juice, bedded in ice, look classically festive heaped in such vessels as copper planters, galvanized tubs, and earthenware containers. Fill a matching container with ice, and stick in a bunch of glasses upside down to frost them. A good part of alfresco dining is showmanship.

ABOVE: *Situated between two rustic yet enticing rocking chairs, a stand filled with ice and cold beverages puts instant refreshment at the fingertips of porch occupants. A simple and thoughtful gesture such as this is sure to go a long way.*

## SIMPLIFIED SERVING

When it comes to serving and removing dishes, particularly when there is a large number of guests, take the easiest route. If a kitchen window opens onto the porch, for example, put it into action as a pass-through. A small table stationed below the window will make it more official and more efficient for helping hands. Guests like to pitch in, so if you're not of the "I'd-rather-do-it-myself school," let them. Using the pass-through, the cook can fix individual plates in the kitchen or easily put out platters of chicken and bowls of pasta salad to be served buffet-style from the table. Such a simple and functional approach epitomizes this type of fair-weather dining.

Portable recruits that can be wheeled in and out of the house, such as an aluminum trolley or a wooden cart, are terrific helpers. They can be used to bring dishes in and out, or they can take up a more stationary role, serving as either a buffet station or a porch bar. Anything you can do to make serving and dining on the porch easier is a short-cut to achieving the relaxation you desire—whether you're surrounded by just a few loved ones or a slew of dinner guests.

BELOW: *Trolleys make willing helpers. The very best can be rolled out to serve as anything from a bar to a dessert station. Use your imagination and pile on the dishes, the extra cups, the cake and the cake plates. Trolleys come in all sorts of materials and shapes. The older wrought-iron or wicker varieties sometimes have more personality. Search for one with character at flea markets and tag sales.*

## FUN FOR THE KIDS

For children, the outdoor dining room is a reprieve. There's more space to wiggle and all sorts of delightful creatures, such as butterflies and fireflies, to watch. Given a special seat on the porch, even finicky eaters improve. Move breakfast or dinner to a table alongside the porch railing, and let the backyard be the entertainment instead of the television. Kid-size furniture makes mealtime more of an event, but any comfortable chair will do when the sun is out and there's a fat gray squirrel to observe. With the proper instruction, children who dine outside readily learn the names of flowers, cloud configurations, and birds. Feed a child's curiosity, and you'll grow a young naturalist. Family dinners on the porch are more leisurely, too. Breaking the routine and moving outdoors enlivens us. Of course, the grand finale to a family dinner outdoors has always been the tinkling bell of an ice cream truck. In lieu of that treat, scoop your own homemade ice cream into cones, sit back with the kids, and watch the goings-on around you.

# Frills

Outdoor dining rooms have it all over indoor ones. The backdrops are already accessorized—an azure sky with clouds in all sorts of fanciful shapes that inspire the imagination, a nighttime sky filled with a dazzling array of stars, birds singing arias from leafy branches, and colorful blossoms in the trees and at ground level. Who could improve upon that? The most uncomplicated meal instantly becomes elevated in status when served alongside a window box brimming with festive blooms. But if your appetite leans toward formal dining, then go ahead and pull out the stops. Alfresco doesn't mean we have to sacrifice style or forgo dressing up. On the porch, silver flatware, good china, and pressed linens are sheer glamour. Why save such accoutrements for indoors only? For many of us, leisure time is enhanced by finally getting to use our finest things—the ones we've kept stored away for far too long. Flowers and shells marry as well with silver and crystal as they do with rattan and wicker. So bring on the French glassware, the rose-colored damask napkins, the candelabra that's been locked in the cupboard waiting to make its debut. With the help of these embellishments, the gathering is bound to take on the spirit of a celebration, whether the menu entails a light and flavorful brioche for breakfast or grilled salmon for dinner.

And that's the point. We're celebrating our free time. Elbows on the table, head in the clouds, we're making every bite and every moment outdoors count. Still, a pretty porch table—one that can stand up to evening clothes—can also be fashioned by using just an Indian bedspread of vibrant multi-colored cotton or a half-dozen straw place mats.

BELOW: *A simple repast becomes a memorable occasion when we splurge on the details. Include an antique cake stand, some delicate cloth napkins, and even a fabulous little figurine you've been saving. The outdoor setting needn't steal all the attention— let the table share some of the glory.*

Both inexpensive alternatives, they each have their own panache. Mix either the bedspread or the mats with silver and they're ratcheted up to courtly. Or allow them to keep their low-key profile, and team them with stainless-steel flatware and cobalt blue goblets that look expensive but aren't. A three-tiered stand of glowing votive candles, a bouquet of tissuelike sweet peas, and you have a ready-in-minutes setting with an appealing stature.

Because nature combines colors and textures all the time, we can too. Mimic her artistry by experimenting: wood-handled flatware with glass dishes, ironstone plates

# THEME PARTIES

EVERY ONCE IN A WHILE, MOVED BY THE PLANETS OR motivated by a special event or holiday, we want to do more than just the usual. Perhaps friends are moving in next door or changing jobs. Maybe someone is starting a new business or retiring. Milestones such as these deserve something a little out of the ordinary. For such occasions, we are justified in going a bit over the top, and the porch is a perfect place to do it. Having a theme enlivens an affair and helps pull it together. How about a Mexican fiesta (translucent colored votives, zesty salsa, and piñatas) for the retirees on their way to a life of kicking back, or maybe a nautical-themed send-off for a couple on their way to some tropical isle to celebrate twenty-five years of marriage. Once you have chosen the theme, the inspiration will follow.

A nautical night, for instance, could be just like taking everyone on a cruise or for a walk on the beach. And the porch doesn't even have to be by the water. Start with the classic yacht club colors of red, white, and blue. Cover the table or tables with starched white cloths that fall to the floor, and then layer smaller cloths on top—red and white stripes, blue and white gingham, or perhaps a bright flag pattern. Roll the flatware for each place setting in a white linen napkin, and tie it with a piece of rope. Post a candle in a hurricane shade at each small table, or string a shipshape line of them down one long table. Instead of a floral centerpiece, collect small model boats in various sizes and use them as table decoration. For a finishing touch, borrow some buoys or oars as props. The highlight of the menu, which could be posted on a nautical-looking board or pinned to a piece of driftwood for everyone to see, might be lobster—stuffed and broiled, for easier eating. If you still fear fingers will get sticky, pass around some finger bowls; a little bit of water, a slice of lemon, and a mint leaf in a small, wide-mouthed bowl are all it takes.

If ships are not your thing, forgo the bright tones, the summer harbor mood, and plan a night as monochromatic and serene as the beach dunes. Set the table with a pale cream-colored cloth and matching napkins. For napkin rings, use broken seashells and push the cloths through the holes. Or wrap a tiny bit of raffia around each napkin, and string on a shell or two as ornaments. Medium-size conch shells, all pink and pearly on the inside, are just right for napkin rings. Scatter sun-bleached starfish up and down the table as though the tide had left them behind, or fill a shallow glass bowl with shells and water and launch a flotilla of small candles on top. String miniature lights or small lanterns along the porch railings and on nearby trees, or place luminarias on the steps to help make the scene more theatrical. Fittingly, the fare should be elegant but simple: perhaps champagne with scallops baked and served in individual shells.

Favors that the guests can tote home at the end of the evening make the night more memorable. For a nautical dinner, such keepsakes might include a boat key ring or a compass tied to each napkin. Flowering plants or herbs in miniature terra-cotta pots, votives, and candy—from chocolates to saltwater taffy—all make fine parting gifts for a porch party. For a children's party, plant a crop of colorful paper or plastic pinwheels among the flowers bursting in the window boxes. Each child can pluck a favorite to take away when the festivities come to a close.

with fragile, hand-etched wine glasses, square Japanese ceramic plates the color of jade with bubbly acrylic goblets. Acrylic plates and glasses are mishap-proof, dishwasher-safe, and come in as many luscious colors as gumdrops. They're also a good alternative in an outdoor setting where kids, or adults for that matter, may be running around in bare feet—no stepping on sharp shards from dropped dishes or broken glasses. To avoid being stuck with a lot of dishes to do, allow one plate per person rather than setting out separate salad and bread plates. Or choose paper plates (the heavy variety, double thickness, or set in a wicker plate holder for stability) and plastic cutlery, which can skyrocket into a festive mode. Using raffia or ribbon, tie up the cutlery in a brightly colored paper napkin and tuck an ivy leaf under the knot. Or wrap plastic cutlery in cloth napkins, attach a flower (zinnias are long-wearing), and lay the grouping in a wire mesh basket where they will be ripe for the picking. An old toolbox—the open kind with a thick handle—will give you the power to tote flatware in and out of the kitchen in one fell swoop.

## NAPKINS

Don't forget the napkins. Napkin art is a bit like origami. The cloth is folded into all sorts of forms, such as exotic lilies, fans, hats, and animals. While artfully shaped linens will jazz up a table, napkins will—unlike soufflés—look just as good flat. Lay them beside or on top of the plates and that's that. If you want to dress them up a little, gather each with a napkin ring—perhaps one that reflects the natural setting. For instance, if you live in a wooded area, try a napkin ring that has a pinecone adornment. Or you might want these table embellishments to reflect a personal passion. If there's nothing you like more than being out on the open sea, use ones with little sailboats. The options are limitless.

Soft cotton napkins launder beautifully and never need ironing, especially if they are going to be rolled around flatware. But napkins also come in scores of other easy-care fabrics. Line baskets with napkins, stow them picturesquely in water goblets, tie them jauntily around wine bottles (which will also help when it comes to pouring), or lay them down diagonally as place mats. For buffet-style meals when guests will be holding their plates on their knees, linen tea towels and bandannas are decorative and more protective than standard napkins, which are usually smaller and daintier. In fact, when you're deciding upon what kind of napkins to use, it's never a bad idea to take into account the food you'll be serving. Chicken salad, for instance,

BELOW: *Naturally elegant, seashells can be used as napkin rings, place card holders, or centerpieces. Scattered here and there or heaped in the middle of the table, these beach trophies create a visual feast.*

will behave nicely with your best linens, but boiled lobster with melted butter translates into lots of thick, heavy-duty paper napkins that can be tossed and replenished without a second thought.

To make sure that you're never caught short, amass napkins, dish towels, and tablecloths in a rainbow assortment of hues. Those with the busiest patterns will camouflage stains (red wine, cranberry juice, spaghetti sauce) best. A collection of clay or ceramic tiles in various colors and patterns, to be used as trivets under hot dishes, will also be useful as well as attractive. Stack them where they can easily be found and grabbed.

## COLORFUL SETTINGS

During daylight hours, the hues we choose for setting our porch tables will undoubtedly garner attention. Selecting colors that work with our slipcovers, shades, or seat cushions will lend continuity to the entire porch. In an outdoor dining room, where nature's colors seem to change every month, there is more fluidity than there is indoors. Look to the color wheel to select complementary tones. Trust your eye, study your beds, borders, and container plantings to get ideas, and then play: lavender, persimmon, cinnamon, red—out on the porch, the table becomes another garden. Dishware patterned with flowers demonstrates an alliance to the garden, but solid colors are often more versatile. To maintain the harmonious ambience of a bare contemporary porch, key the color of these no-pattern dishes to the earth—greens, ivories, blues, and browns.

At night, the mood often shifts into a romantic gear. Japanese paper lanterns (think of John Singer Sargent's famous painting *Carnation, Lily, Lily, Rose*, where the light of the lanterns seems to glow from within the canvas), strings of twinkling all-weather miniature lights, and moonlight transform

OPPOSITE: *In a dazzling white space, each object has sculptural interest: the tall garden obelisks, the iron table, the chandelier. Anchored on a colorful area rug, the dining spot—like an island—lures us to come and join the fun.*

BELOW: *There isn't any stodginess to be found here. Circus colors pervade the outdoor area, covering both the walls and the furniture. The tiled roof casts just enough shade to render dining at the table pleasant, but not so much as to dampen the effect of the boisterous palette.*

a porch. Snowy linens or just an ordinary white cotton sheet used as a cloth (tie the corners bandanna-style) will seem sublimely luminescent in the glow of candlelight. A tablecloth isn't mandated, though, if that's not your taste. Even a narrow white runner—perhaps one of starched linen—will certainly dazzle.

Capitalize on the striking juxtaposition of light and dark with pots and pots of brilliant white flowers, scores of white candles, and white plates. Traditionally, tall candles are set in short candlesticks, short candles in tall candlesticks, but since rules don't hold on the porch, mix everything up the way you would a good bouillabaisse, adding chunky double-wick and triple-wick varieties, votives, and lanterns. Glass holders and hurricane shades will help buffet the wind. For a more wavelike, and thus more natural-looking, stream of light on a long straight table, employ candles of varying heights. Glass shades with a pattern will also yield a more interesting radiance. And out on the lawn, glass lanterns, held aloft on long stakes, can shed small reservoirs of breeze-defying brightness for guests as they arrive and depart. Be generous and set a row of them along the path as well as around the perimeter of the yard or near the steps. If there's a pool, float candles and flowers using unobtrusive platforms of green Styrofoam that will be invisible in the dark.

## ADDED ADORNMENTS

Presentation on the porch should be lighthearted and effortless, and bringing plants and flowers to the table is another method of connecting family and visitors with the outdoors. For spur-of-the-moment decoration, use some florists' wire to fashion a chain of simple greens and swag the front

OPPOSITE: *In anticipation of the night's party, numerous lanterns in a variety of shapes and sizes stand ready. Fitted with candles, a few of these romantic accents can be sprinkled down the center of the table, while others can be scattered around the porch like stars.*

BELOW: *A smattering of votives not only brightens up the dinner table, but also complements the glowing lights that surround the pool. Low bud vases work well with the demure votives, whereas a tall centerpiece might have overwhelmed them.*

# GREAT GARNISHES

IF EVERYONE KNEW THAT THE MIGHTY ROMAN GLADIATORS munched on parsley to give them strength before they went into the arena for battle, there would probably never be another dejected green sprig left on the side of an otherwise empty plate. Many fresh garnishes are packed with such history. A pinch of rosemary was said to ward off witches, a sage leaf to prolong life. It has been claimed that leeks improve the voice and that mint strengthens the nerves. But all that aside, botanical flourishes are visually in sync with alfresco dining. What could be more appropriate than a fresh velvety rose petal or a winsome violet on our sorbet or soup? Nature provides a whole larder full of edible decorations to be tossed into salads or strewn on plates. Start slowly and, above all, serve only those plants or flowers that are edible and that you know are pesticide-free. There's a green or a blossom for every meal on the porch. Take your pick.

* Top an iced coffee cake set on a clear glass cake stand with the wee flower heads of Johnny-jump-ups. The frisky little violets arrive early in the spring.

* Pile spicy orange and red nasturtium blossoms and green nasturtium leaves around the rim of a square ceramic platter filled with shrimp or chicken salad.

* Include a small pinch of minced lemon geranium leaves in your favorite pound cake recipe. Serve the cake on a pink plate with a lemon geranium leaf on the side and a dollop of homemade vanilla ice cream.

* Serve potato salad in a ruby-colored glass or acrylic bowl, and lace with the flowering heads of dill. Or snip off little individual heads to grace a creamy spread for crackers and bread.

* Sprinkle fresh rosemary over lightly boiled new potatoes that have been dressed with olive oil, and scoop them into a pottery dish.

* Arrange a few sprigs of thyme and a tiny dash of fluffy purple chive florets along the sides of a white earthenware platter of cold grilled chicken. (Don't use a whole chive flower as the onion flavor is too powerful.)

of an hors d'oeuvre table that's been draped with a pale cloth. Or imitate a garden path, and scatter rose petals and leaves over a stone-topped table set for dinner.

Not surprisingly, centerpieces often lose some of their importance on a porch. With so much to see all around, fancy trimmings aren't necessary. Three or four perfectly formed heads of white cauliflower or a trio of ornamental cabbages laid on a dark table can be as charming as a vase of daisies; a bouquet of red radishes—misted with vegetable oil to give them some sparkle—can seem as endearing, if not as sweet, as roses. Indeed, some minimal table settings—such as one including chopsticks and shallow celadon bowls—are better left stark, letting the gracefully formed flatware

OPPOSITE: *A rustic, one-of-a-kind table is allowed to shine, thanks to a cloth that covers only part of the surface. Harvest colors, namely deep reds and yellows, appear in both the cloth and the napkins, alluding to the bounty of nature. Two tall candlesticks echo the curvaceous forms of the wrought-iron chairs.*

OPPOSITE: *Natural-looking furnishings on the porch of a rustic log cabin fit right in with the woodland surroundings. So as not to compete with the landscape, a simple bouquet of flowers provides the only decoration on the table.*

and china do the talking. Yet a centerpiece of flowers is never out of place anywhere, and fresh flowers are always luxurious. A few exotic lilies will jump-start a clutch of roadside pickings, and some fresh flowers tucked in among the leaves of a houseplant will be charming and lush. Allow the nature of the event to help you decide on a centerpiece: a bridal shower luncheon would seem empty without flowers, while a weekend dinner for six would work just as well with a low basket of beach stones—the smooth, round sort that everyone at the table will want to reach out and caress before the night is over.

On a long table, using several smaller centerpieces—and perhaps grouping them with votives—will create a cozier feeling (just make sure that there's no threat of leafy tendrils making their way into the flames). Pots of trailing ivy, for instance, will imbue a table with a sensation of lushness. And individual vases filled with just a few posies and arranged in a line will appear as charming as a row of buttons down the back of a summer dress. You could even go so far as to put a bud vase, complete with a flower or two, at each place setting, making each guest feel special. Such diminutive ensembles won't get in the way of people trying to see each other or the surrounding views. If you prefer a large arrangement but are concerned it will cause guests to lean to the left or right or crane their necks in order to talk to people on the other side of the table, position a floral bunch off to the side on a nearby occasional table. Imagine a white pitcher filled with muted mums situated on a trolley cart that also keeps extra drinks on hand, or a metal vase housing a bunch of brown-eyed sunflowers on a table that conveniently holds extra napkins and utensils as well. If your favorite flowers are ones with especially strong scents, you might want to seize the opportunity of an outdoor feast to use them as dec-orative accents; while such potent aromatic blooms as jasmine or tuberoses will overpower the food in an enclosed dining room, they won't have such a strong effect out on the porch.

As a new season approaches, colors change. For example, the soft yellows of sum-mer give way to duskier golden tones. Accordingly, centerpieces move on to the fruits of the harvest. Heap yellow apples—Shizuka, Goldrush, Blushing Golden, Kinsei, or Golden Delicious—in a bowl to create a luminous focal point. Lay a simple track of leaves, nuts, and berries among the plates. Backyards are rich with such decorative accents as the last of the wildflowers, evergreen boughs, ferns, grapes, and grape leaves (if the latter are unsprayed and you want to use them as a garnish on a platter,

RIGHT: *A basketful of luscious oranges can ornament a table as effectively as a more traditional centerpiece, and has the advantage of edibility as well. On this windy beachside porch, the weight of the fruits makes them an excellent alternative to a vase of flowers, which could easily be knocked over by a strong gust.*

OPPOSITE: *Lacy, cast-iron chairs and a matching table are complemented perfectly by a country-style arrangement of daisies, purple coneflowers, and other wayside plants. The cobalt glass pitcher gleams from the table, an inspired choice of container for the lush, informal bouquet.*

soak them in water for a few minutes, roll them in a cotton towel, and store them in the fridge). Take advantage of the branches pruned from shrubs and trees, and lay snippets of them at each place. Or be extravagant and set buckets of them beside the table. Lunch on the porch on a warm autumn day fuels our spirits for the cold months ahead. The rich afternoon light burnishes the table setting as well as the trees and affords one more reason to tarry as long as we can.

On a smaller, country-style porch, personal keepsakes make very effective centerpieces—a school of tiny hand-blown glass fish, porcelain figurines, miniature tins. Colorful and unusual, such additions bring another element of fun. Too whimsical for the interior dining room, like most garden statuary, these collectibles look right at home on the porch. For a special occasion, use them to prop hand-printed place cards and even the littlest dining table will seem very grown up.

## CHAPTER FIVE

# Tending the Porch Garden

ABOVE: *A wicker love seat hunkers down in a leafy corner. Engulfed in flowers and foliage, the sitting area becomes a sweet bower. Bricks and tiles team up to keep the area cool, and they contribute to the garden ambience with their earthy hues.*

OPPOSITE: *Containers bursting with geraniums and petunias enliven the scenery— for both neighbors and those enjoying life on the porch. The floor-level planters make tending and watering easy.*

PORCHES AND CONTAINER GARDENS ARE NATURAL COMPANIONS. In fact, a porch filled with flowers can become a beautiful garden in its own right. The more plants we collect, and the more decorative pots and vintage watering cans we assemble, the richer the scene becomes. Let the rain fall—this protected garden space can be enjoyed regardless of what the weather brings.

After a long and hectic work week, a porch that models itself after a garden can be just the sort of mellow sanctuary we desire. Resting on a porch adorned with plant-filled baskets and window boxes, we're close enough to touch the flowers' silky petals and inhale the fragrance that both soothes and rejuvenates us. If we've grown these flowers ourselves, nurturing them through bad times and good, the pleasure is all the greater. We pick a leaf here and tend a stem there like doting parents fretting over their children. But even the mundane tasks—the small rituals of deadheading, watering, cutting, and clipping—renew us. Each little act is a comforting reminder that a bit of care reaps fabulous rewards.

Gardeners love talking about their plants almost as much as they love tending them, and the bursting of a rosebud or the final emergence of a long-awaited lily is an event that's recounted to all who will listen. From blooms spilling over the rims of hanging baskets to winding vines making their way up trellises to dwarf shrubs set in pots, the porch welcomes all growing things—as well as the contented putterers who seem to accompany them. Hour after hour—though who's watching the clock?— we hover over our plantings, making sure they get all that they need: water, sun,

ABOVE: *The hammock on this porch invites the owner to lie back and admire her handiwork. From this restful spot, a gardener can contemplate future plantings or simply enjoy the bonanza of color and the delightful fragrances.*

fertilizer. Other days, we just sit back and admire the fruits of our labor. The flowers' innocent allure distracts us from our everyday cares. And though occasionally we may grumble about the greedy beetles or some other undesirable pests, we wouldn't consider dismissing our beguiling leafy friends from our lives.

Not only does a porch invite gardening, but this soothing environment encourages dreaming as well. Gardeners spend much of their time fantasizing about the flowers they would like to grow one day, and a porch is the perfect place for germinating ideas. Happily ensconced on a mound of cushions or relaxing in a rocking chair, you can get a good sense of the porch's space and plot out where you might like to add a hanging basket or perhaps some foliage-filled terra-cotta planters. Plus, you can contemplate what to plant in the area surrounding your porch. Your gardening activities are by no means confined to the porch itself. How about some flower beds directly in front of your outdoor retreat? When your porch is elevated a good deal above ground level, the area in front practically cries out to be dressed up with plants. The space around the steps is especially worthy of consideration. A pair of lilac bushes, one on either side of the passageway, will make a welcoming statement to visitors while bringing an element of symmetry to the setting. If you're fortunate enough to have a larger garden within sight of the porch, you can also sit back and envision ways of improving upon the pretty picture that the garden presents. And last but not least, the porch provides a prime spot for simply browsing through gardening catalogs and gleaning ideas. These various ruminations themselves are enough to offer relaxation after a busy day.

But sooner or later, gardeners feel the need to get their fingers in the dirt. Stirred by a warm spring breeze or a whiff of freshly mowed lawn, they head off to the nursery. Across landscapes, urban and rural, bright flowers and lush foliage appear on front porches and back. Gardeners everywhere take delight in their successes, whether they are tending tiny containers of annuals or a vast country garden. After all, a charming window box on a city porch is as satisfying to its nurturer as a towering crop of corn is to a farmer.

## Virtues of a Porch Garden

Sheltered but sunny, a porch is actually a dream location for many plants. And many porches would seem quite lonely without these charming cohorts. With collections of containers on the porch, a savvy gardener is able not only to grow the plants he or she loves, but also to heighten the beauty and appeal of this versatile outdoor room.

And container gardening presents few mysteries. Because the actual gardening space is small, the commitment of time, energy, and cash is also relatively small. You can experiment with new plants, remove specimens that don't perform as you'd hoped, and change the plantings to suit the seasons. A wide range of plants will prosper in pots, as long as their basic cultural conditions are met. While the specific requirements vary from plant to plant, typical needs include good, rich soil with fast drainage, regular watering, and periodic fertilizing. Sun requirements are a bit trickier to calculate. Sun-loving species—most roses, vegetables, and herbs, along with a fair number of flowers— generally need six or more hours of sun a day, an amount that can be difficult to provide in a sheltered area such as a porch. But don't despair if your porch isn't ideal for sun-lovers. Instead, plant these species out in the garden, where they can still be seen from the porch, or use them to line the steps or the outside walls of your porch. Before you purchase a

BELOW: *Thanks to a host of leafy plants, this porch becomes a garden in its own right. With plant-filled containers on the floor, on tabletops, on stands, and in hanging wire baskets, the outdoor room has the feel of a tropical jungle. The verdant foliage complements the bold hues of the tiled floor; flowers are not included as they would only compete with the colorful tiles.*

plant, be sure to check the catalog description or an authoritative plant reference to be certain that you can provide it with the sun and other cultural conditions it needs to survive. Even if you don't have enough light for the flowers and veggies that crave full sun, there are still numerous plants that will thrive in the partly sunny or shady environs of your porch; ferns, primroses, scilla, nicotiana, verbena, and many others find happiness in light shade.

Rotating plantings with the seasons helps tap into nature's cycles and increases the gardenlike atmosphere of your porch. Begin with containers of crocuses, tulips, and hyacinths in spring, change over to long-blooming annuals for summer, and finish with pots of hardy chrysanthemums in autumn. If you are decorating a front porch, where you will be coming and going all through the winter, you might even plant some cold-hardy ornamental cabbages or dwarf evergreens to take advantage of all the seasons. Some bulbs and plants can readily be recycled in the yard, but less frugal and tender-hearted gardeners simply discard the old plants and enlist new ones each season.

There are myriad ways to incorporate plants on the porch. You can hang baskets overhead, allowing tendrils to flow over their edges, or set flower boxes

*ABOVE: On this verdant porch, the ubiquitous coffee table has been replaced with an unusual planter. The hollowed-out log forms an innovative home for assorted mosses and ivies. Playing backup to this centerpiece, potted plants line the window sill and present those inside the house with a gardenlike view. Other container plantings are posted on either side of the sofa, as well as in the corner.*

along the floor's perimeter. The latter can also be mounted on porch railings with the help of brackets. And containers of all sorts can be scattered about on tables and plant stands. Instead of a window box, try lining up a few small decorative pots on a porch window sill. Inventiveness will always pay off. Prop a tall mirror against a wall to reflect and double the effect of lush green foliage.

Don't forget that the porch garden should be as attractive from inside the house as it is up close. Placed optimally, containers will give refreshing views of flowers to interior rooms.

# A Garden of Edibles

Porch gardens needn't be purely decorative. If it is vegetables you desire, tomatoes, salad greens, and squash will do just fine in containers, provided they get the proper amount of sunlight. The construction of your porch and the exposure will affect the amount of light your outdoor room receives. Before you plant, observe the site where you plan to put the vegetables. Note the first hour the spot is fully sunny, then check back every hour (set your kitchen timer!) to keep tabs on the creeping shadows. If you have a location that is fully sunny for six hours or more a day, then you most likely will be able to grow the veggies there. If your porch is too shady, consider suspending baskets of salad greens or other vegetables just outside the porch's overhang or affixing boxes to the outside of the front rail. Just a few inches beyond the sheltering roof can make all the difference. Sun-drenched porch steps can offer another siting option, as long they are wide enough to accommodate a pot or two as well as the foot traffic.

Even the tiniest sunlit porch can host a hanging basket of cherry tomatoes, chili peppers, lettuce, or herbs. Safe from ground-dwelling pests, the lofty tomatoes and lettuce will spill over the basket's sides, forming a giant and delicious bouquet. When mealtime arrives, there's no arduous traipsing through the fields or driving off to the nearest farm stand to collect produce. Instead, you can simply walk across the porch and pick your pleasure.

Let the edible crops grow unashamedly on their own, or soften them with some flowers. Flowers and vegetables mingle in borders, so why not on the front porch? Elegant purple eggplants are sumptuous with blue lobelia all around. And some blooms, such as marigolds, not only make for a pretty picture when tucked among the tomatoes and herbs, all stiff-legged and pert, but also repel parasites. Their pungent but pleasing odor discourages nasty nematodes.

And don't forget the herbs. Like vegetables, herbs generally need a heady dose of sun, so keep the same sun-requirement parameters in mind. If you have the right conditions, consider a whole collection of culinary herbs in individual pots—perhaps some lemon-scented thyme, spicy summer savory, astringent sage, rosemary, cilantro, and dill.

Alas, despite our best intentions some plants, such as asparagus and onions, are best left in the ground. Consult a local garden center or good-quality catalog for the best advice on planting vegetables in containers.

BELOW: *Spicy edible nasturtiums overflow their basket. Hung just outside the kitchen, the flowers are pleasing to porch-sitters and accessible to the cook. The busy chef can easily stop here for a bouquet to scatter atop a salad. Culinary magic!*

RIGHT: *Small though this open porch may be, the billowing flowers make it seem grander. Spiky delphiniums and foxgloves, offset by the cinnamon-colored heads of late-blooming sedum, produce a wave of color and perfume that transforms the wicker rocking chair into a heady garden seat.*

## Flower Power

Flowers, flowers, flowers. As tasty and attractive as vegetables may be, flowers are, and always have been, the porch's crowning jewels. Their sweet and ephemeral nature—here today, gone tomorrow—infuses a space with romance. Start at ground level, and plant faithful tiger lilies or a wave of blue hydrangeas along the front of the porch. Move up the step with pots, set window boxes along the porch's facade, and adorn dining and occasional tables with pots of pretty flowers. You can have as many blossoms as you want—or at least as many as the architecture of the house will allow without appearing completely engulfed.

Coordinating the colors and the textures of your flowers will tame the jungle look and introduce a reassuring sense of harmony. Identical hanging baskets of trailing pink geraniums, for example, lend a porch classic appeal, especially when spaced evenly in a row or arranged in some other sort of symmetrical fashion. Roses that scramble along the railing or up a trellis have a similar but much headier effect. If roses are a favorite of yours, remember that it's possible to grow more than one variety, allowing the two to intertwine. And planting a rose together with another climber, such as the ever-popular clematis, extends bloom time. When the rose is finished, the clematis blossoms will continue to put on a colorful show. Growing roses on your porch affords you the opportunity to gather and dry their fragrant petals and make your own potpourri to give away in decorated sachets (see page 138).

*BELOW: Flowering shrubs lay claim to the base of a farmhouse porch. Up above, hanging baskets take over. The more flowers we pile on, the greater the gardenlike ambience.*

Wax begonias—among our grandmothers' favorites—love hanging baskets, window boxes, and planters alike. Presenting a glorious shower of blooms, they will tumble out of their containers to rave reviews. From snow white to deep red, with lots of fiery oranges and pinks in between, begonias are sure to delight, no matter what color scheme you've chosen.

Pots of annuals, such as petunias or cosmos, can be started outdoors where they can soak up the sun and then shifted to a screened porch when they start to bloom. For blooms that last all season long, plant several containers of cosmos at once, and then rotate them so that they can all have some time in the sun. In warmer climates, commonly overlooked silvery succulents can be striking as window box subjects. Some succulents even trail, creating an effect reminiscent of flowing water—not a bad image on a day when the temperature soars.

Keep in mind that flowers are fine decorating tools. Couple begonias with silver-leafed cineraria and scarlet fuchsias, for instance, to highlight the front of a house. If a more subtle look is desired, paler flowers, such as columbines, hellebores, or lily-of-the-valley, will gladly

step into a corner or fade away against a wall, looking properly pretty but taking a backseat to furniture, fabrics, or rugs. Crowd a window box with brilliant blue lobelia and lipstick red petunias, however, and the whole neighborhood will sit up and take notice. "Hot" colors (oranges, reds, magentas, and bright yellows) warm a shady porch, while "cool" ones (blues, purples, and soft pinks and yellows) will help keep it looking peaceful. Color is a very personal choice. The hues that lift the spirits of some may not be what others would choose. Your porch garden should reflect your personal taste just as strongly as the furnishings do.

Remember that the bigger the mass of a single type of bloom, the greater the visual impact. Picture, for instance, an entire string of neon pink petunias, each fat

OPPOSITE: *Flowers all in the same color range warm this welcoming Victorian. From the bright pink impatiens to a rosy hydrangea, and from jewel-like geraniums to purply chrysanthemums, the plantings complement perfectly the house's intricate paint scheme.*

ABOVE: *Red, white, and blue always make for a striking combination. Here, fiery red blooms in hanging baskets and beds pop against the blue and white facade of the house.*

plant tucked into a small galvanized metal bucket suspended over the porch railing. Even from the end of the street, a display like this will be as eye-catching as the ribbon on a gift package.

When filling a window box, it's usually best to use a few different kinds of plants, each with its own role. The standard "recipe" for such a planting calls for a few trailing plants, some upright kinds to fill the box's middle, and a couple of smaller plants to stagger throughout. Paint the window box to match the home's trim, or perhaps to match the flowers within. The decision is yours—you be the artist.

Flowering vines in containers can easily be trained up porch pillars and posts or along wires to form living green screens. No room for a full-size planting? Nest a small trellis at the back of a window box and plant a single vine. On an old-fashioned back porch, a scampering morning glory with wide-open flowers the color of a summer sky looks as at home as a wooden rocker. On a more contemporary porch in a warm climate, bougainvillea captures the heart. An unpromising city porch transforms into a fragrant bower with the addition of a night-blooming moon vine. Vines of all kinds are traditional porch partners, but you will need to offer the right kind of support. Heavy, woody vines, such as wisteria, need truly solid support, while the delicate tendrils of sweet peas can happily clamber up a few strings. Providing shade and lending romance, vines—slow-growing (climbing hydrangea) or fast (clematis)—soften the architecture and appear to enclose us, fueling the impression of the porch as a sanctuary.

OPPOSITE: *A hanging basket of pastel pink flowers mimics the painted-pink architectural trim of the belvedere. Even the roof ornament is done up in pink. The carefully planned use of color calls attention to the home's details and creates a sense of cohesiveness.*

BELOW: *Wooden trellises stand along the porch and exterior walls, ready to support quick-growing vines. Young climbers will scramble up these simple structures and then onto railings and posts, creating a pretty and effective privacy screen.*

# POTPOURRI, PLEASE

SMALL SACHETS OF HOMEMADE POTPOURRI ARE EASY-TO-make gifts that appreciative recipients can use to scent drawers, sweater chests, or linen closets. All you need to do is sew up small fabric pouches and tuck the potpourri inside. For an even easier approach, lay a small scoop of potpourri in the middle of a pretty handkerchief (antique ones are particularly appealing), gather up the sides to make a small ball-like bundle, and secure with a rubber band. Hide the rubber band with a velvet or satin ribbon, and for an extra flourish, tie on a tiny ornament—an old-fashioned button, a charm, a bead or two, or a sprig of one of the dried herbs or flowers that you've included.

Potpourris are very personal but, in general, each contains three basic ingredients: a base flower, such as rose or lavender, with complementary spices and herbs; an aromatic oil, such as rose or lilac oil; and a fixative, such as orrisroot, sandalwood, or table salt. The oils are included to strengthen the scent of the base flower; add them judiciously, though, as they can overpower. The fixative helps blend the assorted fragrances and retards the evaporation of the oils. If you are going to store the potpourri in a glass container, such additions as tiny pinecones will make the blend look more interesting.

A dry potpourri (there are also moist kinds that call for perfume or brandy) starts with thoroughly dried flower petals and leaves. These can be ones you have grown yourself, ones you have purchased, or a combination of the two. To dry your own petals, spread them on a coarse screen in a cool, dark, dry space or pack the flower heads in silica gel for 3 to 4 days. Many flowers can also be air-dried easily; remove most of the leaves, and hang the flowers upside down in small bunches in a dry, shady spot.

Dried flower petals and foliage are then combined with the spices, oils, and fixatives and stored in a container for several weeks before the sachets are assembled. The recipe that follows will help get you started; it makes enough for at least a dozen small sachets. Containing cloves and cinnamon, this potpourri has a holiday appeal. Feel free to experiment.

### WELCOME HOME PORCH POTPOURRI

*4 to 5 cups dried flower petals*

*3 cups fragrant dried leaves*

*1 tablespoon crushed orrisroot*

*2 or 3 tablespoons dried citrus peel*

*1½ teaspoons crushed anise seed*

*1 tablespoon whole cloves, crushed*

*1 tablespoon crushed allspice*

*3 broken bay leaves*

*1 whole nutmeg, crushed*

*3 broken cinnamon sticks*

*2 broken vanilla beans*

*2 drops each of tuberose, lilac, and patchouli oil*

Pack the petals and leaves loosely in a large container, and mix. Sprinkle in the orrisroot, and add the citrus peel and the spices. Mix again. Scatter the oils on top and seal tightly. Allow the mixture to mellow for 4 to 6 weeks before you put together the sachets. Shake the container regularly to ensure that the mixture stays well blended.

## Shade-Lovers

Too much shade on your porch for any kind of plants, you think? Not possible. Such plants as ferns enjoy the cool, dim corners of a more formal porch, which is probably why the Victorians made such a fuss over them. Their porches, like their houses, had many a murky corner. A stand of lush ferns can be as impressive on a porch as a rose standard. Popular asparagus fern (not really a true fern but a type of ornamental asparagus) has plumes of needlelike foliage that show off well in a hanging basket or a pot. Fill up a four-arm standing plant hanger with baskets of asparagus fern and you'll have your own verdant thicket to filter the light.

ABOVE: *You don't need flowers to jazz up a porch with natural color. Leafy vines winding their way around massive columns will also have a dramatic impact. Here, the foliage and stone join in a timeless marriage that exudes old-world appeal.*

Cheerful impatiens (available in such colors as white, magenta, red, and coral) and vibrant fuchsias, the latter having dangling, earringlike blossoms, will also tolerate their share of duskiness. Other good container plants that will put up with some shade include asters, begonias, bergenia, bellflowers, coleus, creeping jenny, feverfew, geranium, hosta, lobelia, and periwinkle. Check local nurseries for additional suggestions.

Many houseplants that have spent the winter indoors welcome a respite outside on the porch. Combined with pots of bright flowering annuals and perennials, houseplants take on a brand new demeanor. Sprinkle a few pots or urns of tumbling sun-warmed geraniums in with some exotic houseplants bearing spiky foliage, and even a city porch can take on the look of an Aegean terrace.

Topiaries offer an elegant greeting at an entrance. Post a pair at the top or bottom of the porch steps or by the front or back door. Make sure to choose a topiary that suits

BELOW: *Shade-loving impatiens practically take care of themselves. In fact, with a little water, they'll fill out and fluff up, blanketing beds and planters all summer long. The cheerful pink variety shown here contrasts beautifully with the forest green Adirondack-style bench.*

the site. If your steps are shaded for part of the day, select a shade-tolerant species, such as boxwood. (A sunny entrance might be the perfect spot for a topiary of fragrant rosemary or flowering standards of Marguerite daisies.) You could also create a topiary look-alike with a two-level display: put ivy in a pot on the bottom, and set a bunch of bright pink impatiens in an upper-tiered planter that has been lined with sphagnum moss. But be cautious about the wind. A strong summer gust will send the tall, slender topiaries toppling like lightweight aluminum chairs. Window boxes (city ones and rural beauties) can also suffer from too much wind. If this is a problem in your area, choose tough, small-leaved plants that will weather the wear and tear more gracefully, and select rounder, squatter topiaries that won't be bullied.

## Welcoming Wildlife

BELOW: *The hanging basket of petunias found here is a tempting treat for hummingbirds. Suspended just beyond the porch, these flowers draw the diminutive creatures within easy view.*

OPPOSITE: *Plants stands filled with geraniums and hanging baskets containing petunias encourage hummingbirds to visit. A porch swing provides a restful spot from which to observe the wildlife.*

With all these flowers on board, the word will surely go out to the wildlife. Before you know it, you'll have hummingbirds visiting the window boxes and butterflies jetting around the hanging baskets. To encourage the butterflies' presence right into autumn, plant a box or two of nectar-rich blossoms just for them. A butterfly planting, set where it can gather the most sun, might include a mixture of heather, marjoram, sedum (flat-topped, which provides attractive landing spots), and chrysanthemums—all in rosy shades, which are a favorite of these fragile creatures. A highly scented buddleia, or butterfly bush, planted by the porch steps or railing will bring these delicate winged creatures—especially monarchs—in droves as summer begins to wane. Be a good host and supply a shallow birdbath, too, so that the butterflies can have some much needed water.

To entice nectar-sipping hummingbirds, try growing honeysuckle or trumpet vine up a lattice. Or fill your window boxes with red or rosy-colored petunias. A small nectar feeder (available at any bird store) can be hidden among the plants as an additional draw.

You'll find that devoting a little extra effort toward attracting the wildlife will go a long way. A lone butterfly poised on a bud or a bird on a vine can become for many of us a reason to stay very still and reflect. These small moments of observation add up on a porch and help us learn to keep track of time in a new and different way. After just one summer of watching the butterflies, we come to anticipate their

Opposite: *If you want a container that has a little pizzazz, try one with a mosaic design. Here, such a pot rests atop a red table between green shutters. Joined by a vintage watering can, these elements form a charming vignette.*

arrival just as much as we anticipate the bursting of lilac buds or the unfurling of rose petals. The butterflies' brief comings and goings bring us one step closer to the world around us—the world beyond stuffy classrooms and office walls. Watching a glorious swallowtail butterfly flex its wings, we forget our anxieties. And it doesn't matter if you're in an urban or country setting. Birds and butterflies don't discern. They'll come wherever we set out the flowers and feeders. Find a place for them on or near the porch, and just watch, listen, and learn.

## *Pretty Pots*

Today, the choices for containers are as varied as the flowers. They include everything from chic wire baskets to beautifully glazed pottery to imposing stone troughs. Flower boxes alone can be made of a wide array of materials, including redwood, metal, plastic, or woven bark, to name a few.

Keep in mind that the containers you select can receive almost as much attention as what's inside them. Choose your pots and planters with the porch's mood in mind; you might wish to echo the colors of the flowers, or perhaps you'd rather introduce a bit of contrast. Your containers can also step up the atmosphere, lending the porch an exotic aura or a touch of whimsy.

Certain pots are more versatile than others and will work with almost any decor. Terra-cotta pots and planters, for example, are longtime favorites. Their neutral, earthy hue blends with almost every porch style. Available in scores of designs and sizes, they can be displayed singly or grouped together. While terra-cotta has a lot to offer on its own, you could certainly decorate such pots for a change of pace. Perhaps you'd like to sponge or free-hand paint a host of pots in shades that match cushions, furniture, or porch trim.

But terra-cotta is not the only show in town. Ceramic and porcelain pots are pretty, too, and they come in an array of colors and styles, from ones with deep jewellike

# PAINTERLY POTS

Fired red clay terra-cotta pots were produced by hand on a potter's wheel until about the mid- to late nineteenth century, when mechanized pot making came into being. Today, some terra-cotta pots are made by hand, though most are not. Gardeners adore them all for their unique color, their variety of shapes, and their admirable practicality. Even standing empty, waiting for a flowering companion, a terra-cotta pot is a beautiful object. Each one carries the promise of a bloom, and that is often enough for a gardener.

Still, every once in a while, a setting calls out for something more. Painted, sponged, or rubber-stamped, terra-cotta pots on a white porch are like party hats at a six-year-old's birthday. Do up a pot in yellow and orange stripes or in exuberant polka dots. Match the hue of a wicker love seat or mirror the pattern of a cushion. Colorful zinnias love such jazzy containers, as do the more subtle herbs.

Decorating a terra-cot pot is easy even for novice artists. Paint each pot first with a primer, and allow it to dry. Then go to town with acrylic paint: stencil on fish, free-hand paint flowers, or stamp on some leaves. White starfish, blue moons, triangles in a border right around the pot's top edge—the terra-cotta background is definitely user-friendly. Once the paint is completely dry, seal the design with a protective coat of varnish, and let it dry again. The varnish will help make the pot more durable and longer-lasting. When the warm season is over, these painted pots can be moved to a kitchen shelf or to your office to remind you of your summer garden. Assign them the task of holding wooden spoons, wire whisks, or pens.

green or blue glazes to classic blue-and-white Chinese designs. Baskets provide another alternative, and their demeanor is in keeping with the natural look of the outdoors. Brimming with flowers, they can stir up visions of farmer's markets and roadside stands. Put a plastic liner inside the basket to protect it from water, and pop in a potted flower for an instant centerpiece. Those ubiquitous plastic pots are experts at hiding—and not just in baskets. Slip such bland containers inside crocks, antique boxes, tins, or any other sort of decorative vessel for an instant makeover. Half-round baskets or ceramic wall pots, dripping with vinca or stuffed with cosmos and zinnias, make enticing accents when hung on a porch door or wall.

Modern technology has also contributed to gardeners' choices. New ultra-strong, lightweight resin can resemble antique stone or heavy terra-cotta. Resin pots such as these can easily be moved from one spot to another to catch available sun or heat. And portability, in addition to a resistance to weeds, is one of the main benefits of container gardening. This delightful method of growing plants gives you the freedom to move displays wherever and whenever you want (small- to medium-size containers are best). To further help with the shuffling around, you can purchase

OPPOSITE: *No decoration is more natural for a cabin's rustic porch than baskets full of wildflowers. Gather them by the armful from the fields around your house and revel in their exuberant colors and textures.*

LEFT: *Don't be fooled by this trolley's dainty persona. Strong enough to hold a few pots of flowers, the helpful workhorse earns its keep. Painted white to match the chair, the trolley also helps to lighten up the country porch. An assortment of grapevine wreaths displayed on the wall adds textural interest.*

BELOW: *Against a golden, luminescent wall, a gardener has designed an arresting still life with a pair of ornate containers, a shiny vine working its way up a trellis, a brass bell, and a plaster bust. Artfully arranged, the objects capture attention and keep the eye engaged. Fresh-looking white daisies interject some lightheartedness lest we get too serious.*

round galvanized pot trolleys, mounted on a trio of casters, which will move up to 150 pounds (68kg). Gather a group of potted flowers by the steps one day so that the plants get their full dose of sunlight, then cart the lot over to your porch dining area the next. This idea is far from new. Centuries ago, Roman gardeners were known to have set their more tender plants outdoors on wooden planks equipped with wheels so that they could roll them inside whenever bad weather struck.

Keep in mind that square or rectangular containers will gobble up less space on a small porch. Arrange a series of round pots around them. Experiment by staging together different varieties of flowers and vegetables to see which looks the prettiest. And don't hesitate to crowd the plants in the pots. Most container plants like familiarity. If a space opens up, just slip a new variety or two in beside the old. This kind of planting on demand leads to fresh, attention-grabbing mixes of foliage and color.

Even a glimpse of a lone geranium perched in a clay pot or a wall strung with scarlet runner beans can make life suddenly seem sweeter, fuller. Beyond the duties they perform—screening us from our neighbors, providing food or seasonings for the dinner table, offering pleasing views and fragrances—plants and flowers are a joy in and of themselves. The rhythm of seed to shoot to bud to flower is a part of the daily progress and balance of nature. The earth revolves on its axis; the sun comes up and goes down; we plant seeds and they bloom. Often too busy to slow down and take notice of such basic yet awe-inspiring events, we are reminded by our porch gardens of nature's subtle schemes.

## Ambience That Works

With flowers and plants all around, a porch becomes a garden unto itself. When you open the door and venture out to breathe in the fresh air and soak up the scenery, it's a green world waiting for you. The roses you trained on the trellis, the geraniums you set on the steps, and the hanging baskets of trailing ivy all weave their enchanting spells. You can easily sit in this leafy or perfumed retreat and feel transported to another place.

Should you want to heighten the feeling of paradise, there are a number of strategies to employ. A porch is an ideal background for a gardener's ingenuity, and this involves more than just plant life. All sorts of accessories associated with or relating to flowers and foliage can find a new home on the porch. Vases, for instance, possess character, wit, and charm, and many gardeners collect them the way they do seeds. A series of shelves on a porch can hold a group of vases in different heights, shapes, and hues like an array of real blooms in a garden bed. Or they can be linked by some shared trait. Imagine a collection of all-white pottery or a group of tin or hand-painted examples. Showing off these treasures on the porch not only forms an interesting display, but also makes these items readily available when you want to create an arrangement of freshly picked flowers for your outdoor dining or coffee table. Rotate the vases you use for your bouquets so that the shelf display is always changing and each vase gets a turn on the table.

Like vases, stacks of terra-cotta pots can be decorative without any inhabitants. In fact, their sun-baked demeanor can even conjure up images of the Tuscan countryside. Line them up according to size, or stagger them—some tall piles, some short ones, and perhaps one or two individual pots overturned.

BELOW: *A snug front porch calls upon space-saving hanging baskets to bring the joys of gardening to its owners. Making the most of available space, the determined gardeners have stationed two small pots by the door and a basket on the steps. The plants not only allow the owners to engage in a favorite pastime, but also supply cheerful spots of color against the primarily neutral backdrop.*

LEFT: *Terra-cotta pots are beautiful decorative accents in and of themselves. Here, they have been placed on their sides and lined up in rows on a series of shelves. Each pot holds a single apple, either red or green. The alternating pattern results in an intriguing display.*

But these vessels are not the only means of enhancing the garden ambience of a porch. How about hanging up a bunch of straw hats on hooks in a row? Gardening collectibles with a patina of age—weathered birdhouses, tools, ornaments, statuary— will also help enhance your outdoor haven. Set against the porch wall, the textures and faded hues of such treasures will overlap pleasingly like rows of flowers. Keep an eye out for antique watering cans (dents and dings don't matter; imperfection has beauty too), and slowly fill an entire shelf with them. Start a collection of framed seed catalog covers or glass cloches to reflect the light. The real landscape doesn't matter if the one you create on the porch makes you feel like you've wandered into a garden.

## Tools of the Trade

Even the everyday tools gardeners use to care for their plants can add a special note. A group of plant markers or a collection of trowels, perhaps organized in glazed pots or hammered tin bins, provide solace with their own humble appeal. Hang up the bucket, the apron, and the indispensable work gloves. All these can serve as decoration on top of performing their more functional roles.

And speaking of function, you'll need to think about where you'll keep all your gardening implements and supplies and where you'll pot your plants. With a potting bench and a small shallow wood bin of potting soil, you can forge your very own practical garden center right on the porch. Throw in a dry sink, and there is no end to the projects you might carry out all year long.

If the porch is small, wood and steel racks, designed to be nailed to the wall, will make it easy to assemble supplies in one spot—fertilizer, potting soil, a smock. Plunk

BELOW: *This small task area features a portable greenhouse that can be used as a cold frame to get seedlings used to outdoor temperatures before transplanting them in the garden.*

your scissors and pencils (gardeners like to take copious notes) in a flower pot, and use a collection of small stackable baskets to hold string, labels, and clippings of gardens on your must-visit list. Without monopolizing valuable square footage, these setups afford us a home for all our paraphernalia. To carry out potting chores, call upon an occasional table to perform double duty. Drape the table with oil cloth in order to protect it.

For slightly larger porches, there are ready-made, freestanding units that come equipped with such luxurious extras as drawers for keeping seeds and side-mounted

ABOVE: *Boasting painted flower designs, this large table seems a natural spot for arranging fresh or dried cuttings. Sealed with a protective finish, the surface is impervious to water. A flood of natural light makes it easier for the gardener to study each lovely blossom.*

work boxes for such things as assembling pots to fill with spring bulbs. You can also make your own custom potting table or recruit a second-hand table for the job. Any piece that's big enough to hold a few small pots and a bag of potting soil will do. Slide a wooden bin for extra gear underneath the table. A designated work area such as this—no matter what the size—is like having a personal open-air potting shed in which to work. Together with your favorite flowers, you can muck about to your heart's content—potting up bulbs, sowing seeds, pressing leaves and flowers, rooting cuttings, making wreaths, or carving pumpkins. To extend the types of projects you can do, hang a simple wooden dowel with a few hooks from the ceiling and create a drying rack for herbs—perhaps lavender, which repels moths. Tie the herbs in little bunches with raffia, and hang them upside down; provided the weather is warm and arid, you can dry enough lavender to keep yourself perfumed and moth-free all winter long.

In reality, of course, many garden chores are much messier than drying herbs and flowers, so serious gardeners prepare for their tasks. Having a few extra items on hand can help minimize the mess you make. Daily watering (early morning is the best time) is a prime example of an activity that can create disorder—soil overflowing the top of pots and water dripping out the bottom make for a muddy puddle on the floor. The outdoor room, accustomed to rain and wind, is easily cleaned, but these little accidents can almost be eliminated with a bit of forethought. A clay saucer under each pot catches errant drips and flows; mismatched antique saucers or even dutiful plastic trays will also gather water. Shallow copper pans lined with pebbles are great, too; set the copper pans on wide railings, and fill them up with pots.

In rainy areas, or if you keep a lot of potted plants on your porch, forgo the easily stained sisal rug and opt for a vividly painted floorcloth—one you buy or make yourself. Fashioned from a good-size vinyl scrap or a piece of canvas sealed with a protective varnish, the rug will be impervious to the occasional puddle. Paint it with a geometric or floral design, and you'll be walking on color. In warmer climates, porches are often constructed with stone floors, and it's not unusual to find these floors with built-in drains. This means that gardeners can even drag out a hose for the big jobs. Gravel floors are also willing to work, but unlike ones made of stone or cement, they can't be tidied up with a good sweep.

If you're building a new house and are a serious gardener, give special thought to the porch floor and ceiling. A skylight in a porch roof can transform a formerly

OPPOSITE: *A bent-twig frame reminiscent of Elizabethan garden edgings makes an excellent drying rack for bunches of flowers and herbs. Once the plants have been tied and arranged, the rack can be moved to a dark, dry, well-ventilated place so that they can dry without fading. The classic garden bench and brick flooring are practical in a space that will be used both for garden chores and for relaxing.*

dark space into a prime growing location. And the good news is that skylights are relatively inexpensive and easy to install. During the day, the extra light from above speeds along the herbs and keeps the tomatoes ripening. At night, such a window is a personal gateway to the stars.

## Garden Furniture

Flowers and plants make all sorts of porch furnishings look prettier—how could they not? A pot of long-blooming agapanthus beside a rattan chair is like a jolt of blue, heaven sent. Once we've assembled our pots of flowers, we want to just sit back and appreciate them. Any chair next to a fragrant rose is going to be a seat fit for a king, but certain pieces do seem to play off the charm of a garden especially well. Twig chairs,

BELOW: *Lucky is the individual who gets to relax in this wicker rocker. Situated next to a matching wicker table crowded with merry geraniums, the occupant gets to savor the blooms' natural beauty up close.*

for example, have an obvious affinity with plants, thanks to the branches out of which they're crafted. Wicker, painted white or green, makes an excellent foil for flowers and foliage, as do dainty wire chairs that echo the tendrillike form of plant growth. Often, however, fabulous combinations of furniture and plants are rather unexpected, so be willing to experiment. A Mission-style rocker next to a wooden planter brimming with climbing black-eyed Susan vine is a match that one gardener stumbled upon, but it happens to be an effective one. The dainty, dark-eyed, sunshine-yellow flowers and the stocky, no-nonsense chair balance each other out like yin and yang.

It is always a nice idea to use furniture and flowers as partners on the porch. For instance, pairing painted furnishings with blooms in matching or complementary hues can create pleasant vignettes. Purple clematis next to a blue bench, or perhaps pink begonias next to a yellow rocker? The color combinations can dazzle and enchant. Add a few pillows in a fabric that replicates the flowers and you've created a restful nook for relaxing with favorite garden books or a pretty place to have coffee with a friend.

By selecting fabrics that mirror the plantings for slipcovers, chair cushions, and hammock pillows, you increase the number of flowers in your porch garden. Festooned with blooms, the furniture will appear as though it has sprung from the garden. When you succumb to the pleasure of rocking in the swing or reclining on

ABOVE: *Foliage and flowers are joined by romantic floral upholstery to enhance the gardenlike mood of this porch. While the architecture is grand, wicker furnishings bring a natural, down-to-earth feel to the space. Heavy pots—filled with flowers that match the blooms on the seat cushions and sofa— line up on the balustrade, while leafy plants pop up here and there throughout the porch.*

the glider, you'll feel embraced by the plethora of blossoms around you. And a floral tablecloth can create the sensation of picnicking in a meadow of wildflowers.

Of course, furnishings designed to take up residence in a full-fledged garden can also infuse your porch with garden overtones. These can be made of wood or metal. Picture a white-painted wrought-iron table and matching chairs with airy designs. Peeling paint, even rust, have their place in this casual environment. If you uncover an antique wrought-iron love seat that's worn and weathered and you find you like the time-honored look, keep it. A distressed seat such as this paired with a vase of blowsy pink roses beside it can create a scene of ultimate romance and suggest to all who sit there a sort of old-time grandeur. Incorporating furnishings and flowers that live in harmony with one another can only heighten the peaceful feeling of relaxing on the porch.

OPPOSITE: *Aside from actual plants, nothing pumps up a garden aura more effectively than floral-patterned upholstery and slipcovers. Available in all sorts of appealing designs, such fabrics imitate real life. Although traditionally coupled with wicker, floral patterns work well on all types of furnishings.*

ABOVE: *White wicker furniture not only lightens up the heavy brick backdrop but contributes a garden ambience to this porch. Potted plants are scattered along the edge of the porch, while additional plantings cover the area directly below.*

# SOURCE DIRECTORY

## OUTDOOR FURNISHINGS & ACCESSORIES

Casablanca Fan Company
761 Corporate Center Drive
Pomona, CA 91768
(888) 227-2178
*Ceiling fans.*

The Company Store
(800) 285-3696
www.thecompanystore.com
*Table linens.*

Country Casual
(800) 284-8325
www.countrycasual.com
*Outdoor furnishings and planters.*

Cumberland Woodcraft Company, Inc.
P.O. Drawer 609
Carlisle, PA 17013
(800) 367-1884
*Resin Adirondack-style furniture.*

Design Toscano
17 East Campbell Street
Arlington Heights, IL 60005
(847) 255-6760
*Replicas of historical garden sculptures, including urns, angels, and gargoyles.*

Fran's Wicker and Rattan Furniture
295 Route 10, Dep. 346
Succasunna, NJ 07876
(800) 531-1511

Frontera
(800) 762-5374
www.frontera.com
*Contemporary outdoor furniture and accessories.*

Giati Designs, Inc.
614 Santa Barbara Street
Santa Barbara, CA 93101
(805) 965-6535
*Teak furniture, sun umbrellas, and exterior textiles.*

Hunter Fan Company
2500 Frisco Avenue
Memphis, TN 38114
(901) 743-1360
*Ceiling fans.*

Marion Travis
P.O. Box 1041
Statesville, NC 28687-1041
(704) 528-4424
*Oak porch swings.*

Martha By Mail
(800) 950-7130
www.marthabymail.com
*A full range of furniture and accessories, from steel garden chairs and wirework window boxes to birdhouses.*

Marty Travis
R.R. 1, Box 96
Fairbury, IL 61739
(815) 692-3336
*Shaker-style seed boxes.*

Old Hickory Furnishing Company
403 South Noble Street
Shelbyville, IN 46176
(800) 232-2275
*Rustic furniture.*

Orvis
(800) 541-3541
www.orvis.com
*Rustic twig furniture and weather-resistant wicker.*

Pompeian Studios
90 Rockledge Road
Bronxville, NY 10708-5208
(800) 457-5595
*Italian hand-forged wrought-iron tables, chairs, consoles, settees, gliders, and more.*

Rocket Dog Studio
114 North Main Street
Providence, RI 02903
(401) 273-2012
*Cast stone, ceramics, sculpture.*

TideWater Workshop
(800) 666-TIDE
www.tidewaterworkshop.com
*White cedar furniture.*

Triconfort
12200 Herbert Wayne Court
Suite 180
Huntersville, NC 28078
(800) 833-9390
*Teak, lacquered resin, and aluminum garden furniture.*

Vermont Outdoor Furniture
(800) 588-8834
www.vermontoutdoorfurniture.com
*White cedar porch swings, Adirondack chairs, tables, benches.*

Wicker Warehouse
195 South River Street
Hackensack, NJ 07601
(800) 989-4253
www.wickerwarehouse.com
*Brand-name wicker furniture and accessories.*

Winston Furniture Company
160 Village Street
Birmingham, AL 35124
(205) 980-4333
*Casual furniture for outdoor use.*

Woodard
317 South Elm Street
Owosso, MI 48867
(517) 725-2290
*Wrought-iron furniture.*

Wood Classics
P.O. Box 291
Gardiner, NY, 12525
(914) 255-7871
*Everything from benches to porch swings, available fully assembled or in kits.*

## CUSTOM PORCHES, DECKING, AND ARCHITECTURAL ELEMENTS

Archadeck
(888) OUR-DECK
www.archadeck.com
*Custom decks and porches.*

Cinder Whit & Company
733 Eleventh Avenue South
Wahpeton, ND 58075
(800) 527-9064
*Porch posts, balusters, spindles, and more.*

Heritage Vinyl Products
1576 Magnolia Drive
Macon, MS 39341
(800) 473-3623
*Maintenance-free fencing, decking, and garden products.*

Vintage Wood Works
Highway 34 South
Quinlan, TX 75474
(903) 356-2158
*Wooden screen doors, porch doors, and decorative porch trim.*

PLANTS, BULBS, SEEDS, AND
GARDEN ACCESSORIES

Bittersweet
30 West Main Street
Wickford, RI 02852
(401) 294-6990
*Garden-style ornaments, watering
cans, sprinklers, planters, and pots.*

Dutch Gardens
www.dutchgardens.com
(800) 818-3861

John Scheepers
23 Tulip Drive
Bantam, CT 06750
(860) 567-0838
www.johnscheepers.com

McFayden Seed Co. Ltd.
Box 1800
Brandon, Manitoba R7A 6E1
Canada
(204) 571-7500
www.mcfayden.com

Smith & Hawken
(800) 940-1170
www.smithandhawken.com
*Mail-order gardening supplies.*

W. Atlee Burpee & Company
300 Park Avenue
Warminster, PA 18991-0003
(800) 888-1447
*Mail-order flower, herb, and vegetable
seeds and plants.*

White Flower Farm
Litchfield, Connecticut
(800) 503-9624
*Mail-order plants, tools, and
containers.*

# PHOTO CREDITS

Beate Works: ©Grey Crawford:
pp. 41, 92, 103

©Steven Brooke: pp. 89 (Scott
Merrill, Architect), 124

©Sonja Bullaty: pp. 43, 157

©Bumgarner/Photo Network:
p. 128

©Corbis: pp. 12, 16, 81

©Deanne Cunningham: p. 62 (James
Schoenle, Gardener)

©Carlos Domenech Photography:
pp. 22 top (Randy Williamson,
Architect), 22 bottom (Randy
Williamson, Architect), 25 top, 34,
36 (Jeffrey Howard Interiors), 38,
39, 64, 72 (designed by Pilar Larraz),
73, 129 (designed by Luciano Alfaro
III), 139 (designed by John Telleria)

Elizabeth Whiting Associates: pp. 61,
91, 94, 99 top, 107, 108, 126, 154

©Phillip H. Ennis Photography:
pp. 35 top (designed by Richard
Neas), 35 bottom (designed by
Richard Neas), 58 (designed by Four
Seasons Greenhouses), 96 (designed
by Nancy Corzine), 150 (designed
by Patricia Kocak), 156 (designed by
Peter van Hattum)

©Derek Fell: pp. 65, 131

©Tony Giammarino: pp. 21, 34, 77
(designed by Susan C. Kipp)

©Tria Giovan: pp.15, 37, 53, 67, 75,
99 bottom, 115, 145, 147 bottom

H. Armstrong Roberts: ©Paul Avis:
p. 133; ©Blackfan: p. 113; ©M.
Gibson: p. 135; ©F. Gordon: p. 40;
©D. Petku: p. 33; ©K. Rice: p. 97;
©F. Sieb: p. 127; ©A. Teufen: p. 15

©Nancy Hill: pp. 110 (designed by
Grant Larkin), 111 (designed by Jan
Burket), 116 (designed by Stephanie
Stokes Inc.)

©Home Magazine: p. 18

International Stock Photo: ©Stefan
Lawrence: p. 140

©Jessie Walker Associates: pp. 5,
19, 28 (Martindale Inn), 44, 45
(designed by Marjorie Busch),
47, 82, 104 (designed by Joanne
Boardman), 112, 130 (designed by
Anita Locke Phillpsborn, Allied
ASID), 142 (designed by Marjorie
Busch), 147 top (designed by
Jan Carroll), 149 (designed by
Gaye Bowers)

©Michael Jensen: p. 55 (Prentiss
Architects)

©Dennis Krukowski: p. 63, 93, 100,
141

©Angelo Lomeo: p. 80

©J. Paul Moore: p. 48 (designed by
Debbie Gregory)

©Keith Scott Morton: pp. 59, 70
bottom, 83, 90, 106, 155

New England Stock: ©William
Johnson: p.14; ©Stefan Lawrence:
p. 79; ©Lou Palmieri: p. 134; ©Jim
Schwabel: p. 2; ©Michael Shedlock:
p. 143

©Franklin and Esther Schmidt:
pp. 88, 109, 151

©Brad Simmons Photography:
pp. 8, 25 bottom, 46, 49, 56, 60, 70
top, 71, 74, 101, 123, 125, 146, 148,
152

Spectrum Stock: p. 132 ©Bert
Klassen, p.137 ©Lorraine Parow,
p.144 ©Norm Piluke

©Tim Street-Porter: pp. 13, 23, 31,
40, 42, 69, 76, 78, 117, 119

©Brian Vanden Brink: pp. 6 (John
Morris, Architect), 9 (Rob Whitten,
Architect), 17 top, 17 bottom, 24,
26, 27(Scott Simons, Architect), 29
(Quinn Evans, Architect), 30 (John
Gillespie, Architect), 32 (Weston &
Hewiston, Architects), 50 (John
Gillespie, Architect), 52, 54, 84 top
(Orcutt Associates, Architects),
84 bottom (Orcutt Associates,
Architects), 85 (Orcutt Associates,
Architects), 102 (Weatherend
Furniture), 136

©Dominique Vorillon: pp. 10
(designed by Barbara Drake), 11
(designed by Barbara Drake), 57
(designed by Wendy Michael), 66
(designed by Barbara Barry), 86, 95,
98 (designed by Michael Lee), 105,
118 (designed by Madeline Stuart),
121 (designed by Elaine Paul)

# INDEX

Awnings, 99, *99*, 100

Baskets, hanging, 126, 129, *129*, 130, 131, *131*, *136*, 137, *137*, 141, *141*, 148, *148*

Benches, 18, *18*, 39, *39*, 40, *42*, 43, 50, *51*, 70, 101, *101*, 102, *102*

Cabinets, 93, *93*, 106, *106*

Chairs, 100–104
    Adirondack, 40, 41, *41*, 43, *43*, 71, 122, *123*
    aluminum, 34
    bentwood, 104
    director's, 49, *49*, 104
    folding, 97
    garden, 102
    rattan, 41
    rockers, 8, *9*, 12, *13*, *26*, 27, 30, *31*, 35, 38, 39, 71, *73*, 80, *80*, 84, *85*, 105, *105*, 154, *154*
    twig, 83
    wicker, *8*, 33, *33*, 34, *36*, 39, *39*, 66, *66*, 71, *72*, 77, *77*, 80, *80*, 90, *91*
    Windsor, 32, 93, *93*
    wing, 105, *105*
    wrought-iron, 99, *99*, 102

Chaise longues, 40, 60, *61*, 69, 105

Chests, 53, 77, *77*, 104, *104*

Color, 33, 43–44, 71, 100

Columns, 15, *15*, *16*, 17, *17*, 95, *95*, 139, *139*

Containers, plant, 63, 65, 126–157
    flowers for, 132–137
    materials, 144–148
    self-watering, 65
    tools for, 150–154

Cushions, 39, 70, *70*, 100

Dining, 90–125

Drapes, 34, *35*, 66, *66*, 67, *67*, 99

Entertaining, 106–124

Fireplaces, 27, *27*, 40, *40*, 55, *55*, 58

Floorcloths, 32, 97

Floors
    painted, 34, *35*, 71
    stone, 14, *14*, 58
    wood, 18, 28, *28*

Fountains, 77, 78, *78*

Furnishings, 35–43
    arrangements, 30–33, 40, 43, *43*, 52, *52*
    child-size, 53, 110
    fabrics, 45, 48, 99, *99*
    garden, 154–157
    lightweight, 34
    mobility of, 34
    oversize, 38, *38*, 69
    painted, 40
    polypropylene resin, 38
    rattan, 56, *57*, 71
    weatherproof, 39, 100
    wicker, *8*, 21, *21*, 33, *33*, 34, *34*, *36*, 38, *38*, 40, 48, *48*, 63, *63*, 71, *72*, 77, *77*, 80, *80*, *82*, 83, 84, *85*, 90, *91*, 99, *99*, 154, *154*, 155, *155*, *156*, 157, *157*

Hammocks, 70, *71*, 83, 128, *128*

Hot tubs, 87, *88*, 89, *89*

Latticework, 18, 95

Lighting, 54–57
    all-weather, 117
    candles, 56
    chandeliers, 54, 55, *116*, 117
    lanterns, *118*, 119, *119*
    sconces, 56

Linens, *82*, 83, 96, 106, 115, 117, 119

Pergolas, *42*, 43, *94*, 95

Planters, 63, *63*, 87, 100, 130, *130*, 142, *143*

Porches
    back, 79, *79*, 80, *80*
    contemporary, 41
    dining on, 90–125, 95–98

enclosed, 58, *58*, 59, *59*, 89, *89*, 100, *100*, 105, *105*
    formal, 34, *35*
    front, 33, 84, *84*, 148, *148*
    gardening on, 126–157
    maintenance, 59
    private, 60–89
    screened, 50, *50*, 58, 71, *73*, 81
    seaside, 18, 25, *25*, 124, *124*
    seasonal arrangements, 46–47
    second-story, 12, 23, *23*, 81–86
    side, 79
    sleeping, 81, *82*, 83
    small, 30, *31*, 39, 97
    spa, 87–89
    wraparound, 17, *17*, 23, *23*, 87, *88*, 89, 95

Privacy, 60–89

Railings, 15, *15*, *16*, 17, 49, 70, *70*, 84, *84*

Rugs, 33
    area, 32, *32*, *116*, 117
    cotton, 32
    hooked, 104, *104*
    natural-fiber, 90, *91*
    placement, 97
    sea grass, 32
    sisal, 32

Screens
    fabric, 66, 68
    folding, 67–68, 97
    hanging plants as, 66
    lattice, 95, 97
    movable, 87
    plantings as, 62, *62*, 63, *63*
    rice-paper, 87
    wooden, 68

Shades, 66, 99, *99*, 100, *100*

Slipcovers, 45, 48, 104

Sofas, 33, 40, *40*, 105, *105*

Styles
    Arts and Crafts, 21, 54, *54*, 102
    classical, 12, *16*, 17
    Colonial, 104

contemporary, 23
    country, 104, *104*, 124
    Craftsman, 18, *18*
    Gothic, 12, *13*, 15
    Greek Revival, 15, *15*, 41
    Moroccan, 10, *10*
    Queen Anne, 15
    Shaker, 104, *104*
    Spanish Colonial, 15
    Spanish Revival, 41
    traditional, 95
    Victorian, 21, *21*, 23, 40, 104, *134*, 135

Swings, 24, *24*, 69, 70, *70*

Tables, 28, *29*, 100–104
    coffee, 32, 39, *39*, 56, *57*, 70, 102, *103*
    dining, 32
    end, 71
    folding, 70, 97
    glass, 34, *34*, 38, *38*, 71, 99, *99*
    nesting, 49
    picnic, 101, *101*
    round, 32, 34, *35*, 70, 101, *102*
    side, 34, *37*, 102
    wicker, 154, *154*
    wrought-iron, 99, *99*

Trellises, 63, 95, 126, 137, *137*

Verandas, 20, 95

Wicker, 21, *21*
    chairs, *8*, 33, *33*, 34, *36*, 39, *39*, 66, *66*, 71, *72*, 77, *77*, 80, *80*, 90, *91*
    furnishings, 33, *33*, 34, *34*, *36*, 38, *38*, 40, 48, *48*, 63, *63*, 71, *72*, 77, *77*, 80, *80*, 84, *85*, 90, *91*, 99, *99*, 154, *154*, 155, *155*, *156*, 157, *157*
    tables, 154, *154*
    weatherproof, 35

Wildlife, 142–144

Window boxes, 63, 65, 79, *79*, 84, *84*, 126, 137, 141

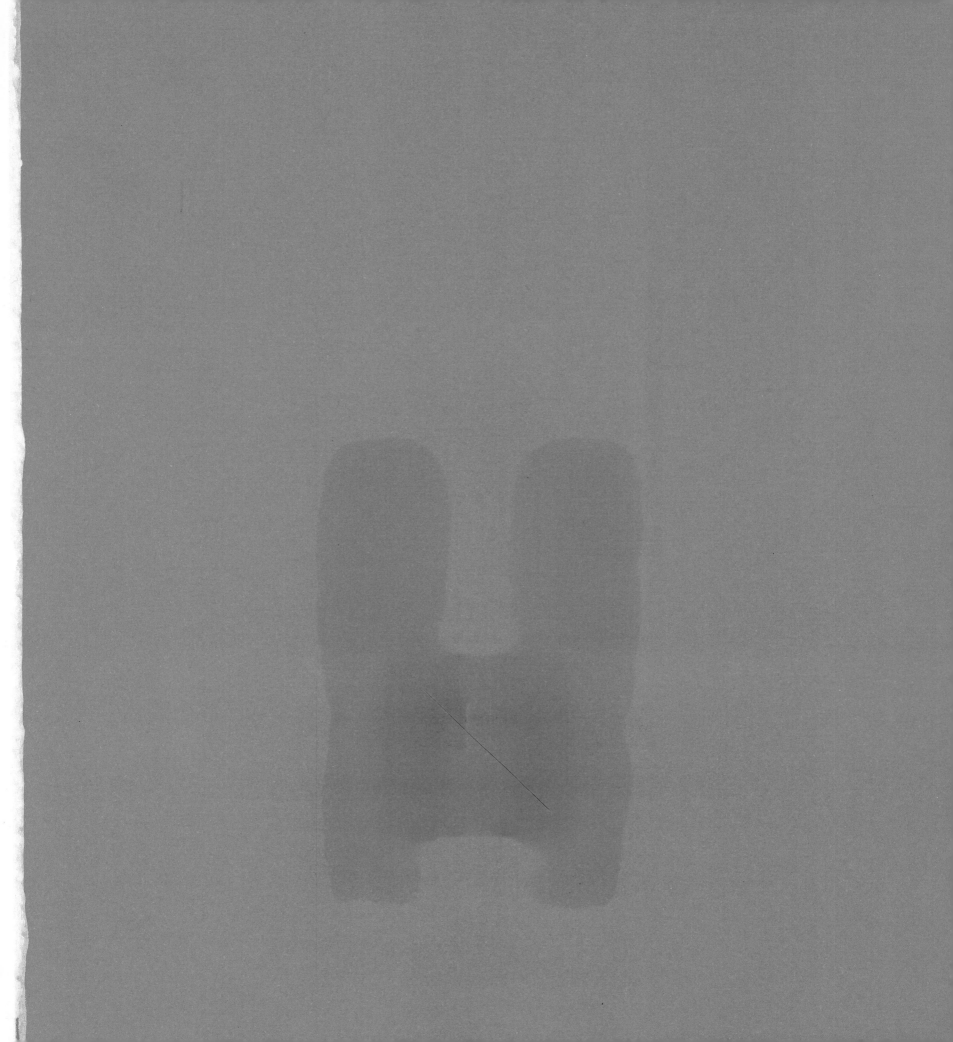